HAMLET
AND THE ETERNAL
PROBLEM OF MAN

Arthur G. Davis

Assistant Professor of English
St. John's University   Redmen

SJU #1

1 9 6 4

ST. JOHN'S UNIVERSITY PRESS   •   NEW YORK

Published by St. John's University
in celebration of the
400th Anniversary Year
of the birth of William Shakespeare
1564-1964

8095

Library of Congress Catalog Card Number: 64-8691

TO GISELA

PREFACE

In writing this book I have taken definite positions on two important controversies, both of which materially affect our view of Hamlet's character: first, Hamlet at no time is insane; and second, Hamlet had an obligation to avenge the murder of his father above and beyond mere personal vengeance.

Insanity may be taken to mean anything from emotional instability to severe mental derangement. Whatever terms may be technically proper, I will leave to the experts in the field of psychiatry. In the following pages, however, I hope to show that Hamlet's emotional fluctuations — severe though they may be at times — do not constitute unsoundness of mind. Dr. Max Huhner, in his work *Shakespeare's Hamlet*,[1] convincingly demonstrates that from a medical viewpoint Hamlet was never insane, either before or during the action of the play.

As to the second point, the obligation of revenge, it must not be forgotten that Hamlet was the highest representative of the law in Denmark. Technically, let us admit, the right of Claudius to the throne was sound enough had he attained his position by lawful methods. But the fact remains that he has become king through regicide. And who but Hamlet, the only son of the murdered king, holds a legitimate claim to the throne? Claudius's black crime poses the immediate need for an agent of retributive justice. Whoever is given such a role must have the greatest legal and moral justification for assuming it.

Furthermore, avenging the murder is not Hamlet's idea but the ghost's. The Prince is simply responding to what he has been specifically ordered to do. Now, when we consider what the ghost represents we become involved in certain Catholic beliefs which not everyone will grant. For instance, from the ghost's words in Act I, Sc. 5 we may safely infer that it is in Purgatory.

> I am thy father's spirit,
> Doomed for a certain term to walk the night
> And for the day confined to fast in fires
> Till the foul crimes done in my days of nature
> Are burnt and purged away.

This would indicate that the elder Hamlet has already appeared before the judgment seat and been deemed worthy of heaven after submitting to a period of temporal punishment. He is not condemned to eternal damnation but is still on the right side of the law of God. He neither could nor would return to earth to perpetrate evil, nor to set anyone else on to do it.

Of all the ghost's in Shakespeare this one is the hardest to dismiss as a figment of anyone's imagination. Its reality, even before Hamlet knows of its existence, is established beyond any question: Marcellus, Bernardo, and Horatio have seen it. That it is an entity and not a figment of "antipathies groping for justification" places the responsibility for Hamlet's avenging role above and beyond the world in which he lives and, additionally, on a firm moral basis.

To avoid this conclusion one must seek explanations which, though plausible at first glance, fade away as we begin to examine them. One explanation is that the ghost is a devil. Hamlet himself entertains this suspicion, though he later insists he would "take the ghost's word for a thousand pound!" Both before and after Hamlet's conviction on this point, however, we are well aware that the ghost has not uttered a single lie and that, in spite of its bitter denunciation of Gertrude's infidelity, it expresses the kindliest reliance on heaven and her own conscience to work ultimately toward her spiritual regeneration. Nothing in the outcome of the play can possibly justify the notion that the ghost has been a corrupting influence or an instigator of evil designs.

We can easily avoid the interminable discussion this question would entail by pointing out something not generally recognized. It is too often assumed that Hamlet is forced into the role of hired assassin and must dispatch his uncle in some perfidious manner. Such a role is its own condemnation; the conflict between this role and the lofty character of the youth who must assume it is apparent at a glance. Harold C. Goddard elaborates at great length upon this conflict and concludes, logically enough, that the killing of Claudius is an evil act which Hamlet instinctively desires to avoid.[2] As convincing as Goddard is, however, his entire thesis rests on two unwarranted suppositions: first, that the ghost orders Hamlet to kill, and second, that the killing would be insidiously motivated and viciously carried out. Both notions have some merit. Hamlet himself talks as if hatred ought to guide his actions. At one point he has an opportunity to stab his father's murderer in the back, contemplates it for a moment, but turns away. (In the final scene he does in fact stab Claudius to death.)

On the strength of these and some lesser points of evidence, many believe that the ghost intended the vengeance to take the particular form of stabbing. Nothing could be wider of the mark. I will say more on this in its proper place because Hamlet's character depends in part upon the fact that he himself, not the ghost, begins to conceive this duty in a way unfit and improper, even degrading. Never does the ghost say or even imply how Hamlet should punish his uncle, except for the all-important injunction

> But, *howsoever thou pursuest this act,*
> Taint not thy mind . . .

If, through some imperfection or error of judgment, Hamlet chooses, or at least seems to choose, a method we find reprehensible, the wrong cannot be imputed to that mysterious figure that issues out of eternity and solemnly adjures Hamlet to keep his mind pure.

I would rather postpone further discussion just now so as not to anticipate what I will take up later in more detail. But the point should be clear that neither Hamlet's behavior nor the circumstances of the entire play will support the view that the deed enjoined upon the Prince was morally wrong or legally insupportable, or that he shrank from his duty only because of innate gentleness or a subconscious inhibition.

One word more about the method of the study. I have not studied the play — based on the G. B. Harrison text — in the chronological order of acts and scenes. What I have done is to examine Hamlet's character in a number of different connections, doing my best to handle each one by itself. This meant that I had to return to scenes previously discussed in the light of some other side to the main character. The choice lay in discussing one part of the play in all its meanings, and then moving on to another; or taking individual considerations and treating them separately, and so having to return to certain parts of the play several times. For this reason I ask the reader to withhold his judgment until I have concluded all.

This method is certainly not the way we ought to read or hear *Hamlet*. My wholehearted agreement is with those who maintain that the play should unfold before us, scene by scene, in exactly the manner it unfolded for Shakespeare's audiences. No scene should be digested in relation to what we anticipate is going to happen in future scenes. Nevertheless, any great work of art demands analysis, which cannot always proceed in the precise chronological order of the action. The better we know the play the better will we enjoy it in the performance. Any loss of surprise is a small price to pay for a deeper awareness of the manifold significances of each action as it occurs. We dissect a play not to leave it in pieces but to see it more clearly in its entirety.

Arthur G. Davis
New York, 1964

TABLE OF CONTENTS

I
THE UNIVERSALITY
OF HAMLET

If Hamlet can be so many things to so many people and if he can reflect the light of each age, he must indeed contain some pure unchanging essence to which the greatest complication of angles and sides eventually leads. It is the world that changes, not this mysterious young prince who attracts all and has something to say to each. Indeed, what we perceive in Hamlet lies in a text forever fixed, itself rigidly permanent, though men have read it differently. In addition, men have always sought to read the whole of Hamlet's character, and not some part that might be supposed to strike a special response. Two men living in two different centuries may see very different Hamlets, but each looks at the entire man — or at least makes the effort to do so — and concludes from all he sees. A living character would be less remarkable for undergoing such a change. In a fictional character an eternal succession of changes must appear miraculous.

The magnetism of Hamlet, therefore, is more than the attractiveness of a riddle. He is much more than an enigma which everyone has so far failed to solve. He is the eternal mirror in which each man may see himself, and the observer who mistakenly sees what is not really in Hamlet but in himself may be closer to the truth than a more detached observer who is coldly correct in his analysis. Scholarly correctness, whatever it may assist us to learn, remains outside the inner mystery, a mystery the intuitive man has sensed, whether or not he sees imperfectly. And if he is in danger of seeing imperfectly, let him be aware of reasonable cautions in advance. Let us not trust intuition too far. It is a refreshing change, a pathway to truth, and one may become so intoxicated with it as to cast aside all analysis. But anyone who demands truth will find his intuitions relatively easy to scrutinize once the heat of powerful feeling has subsided and what he has felt remains as a sacred religion to be guarded yet examined. It is next to impossible to conjure up powerful feelings as a result of academic findings only.

The caution against seeing oneself in Hamlet is, of course, a well established one. Many people in studying the character of the prince have succeeded — unawares, no doubt — in identifying him with themselves. Coleridge's famous dictum, it is said, is not true of Hamlet but certainly true of Coleridge. And Goethe's is not true of Hamlet either but true of Goethe. Hundreds of similar examples might be adduced to prove the point. The answer, however, may not be in keeping oneself out of Hamlet — a difficult and unnatural thing to do — but in seeing oneself more clearly. Coleridge may indeed have looked at Hamlet and seen Coleridge, but how well did he see

Coleridge? His self-analysis, however subconscious — indeed, because it *was* subconscious, perhaps — could certainly have been incomplete. And if incomplete, the real nature of himself and the character he was attempting to interpret escaped him except at those points that loom out of obscure depths which only the light of philosophy can penetrate.

Only a more comprehensive concept of mankind can begin to provide us with answers. Unfortunately, the flight from tradition, the revolt against dogmatic definitions by which man has learned the secrets of his own soul, have brought in their wake all the disunion of intellectual waywardness. The fads of various kinds of esotericism follow one another as the pendulum swings not merely back and forth but in every conceivable direction, each upsurge a flash of something interesting and to some extent true. But we cannot put together the contradictions of the ages into a unified truth any more than we can make sense out of the discord of Hamlet's varying appeal to those ages. We must see through both. The whole is, in each case, more than the sum of its parts.

Hamlet is the product of a culture that knew a truth beyond all the confusions and diversities of life. It is certainly logical to look at him in terms of that truth. If it be insisted that we today are too far away from it, then we must be too far away from Hamlet as well, who would survive as a relic of the past and nothing else. But the appeal of Hamlet to our modern world would refute such a notion at every turn. The fact is — and it cannot be repeated too often — we are as attracted to him as any age has ever been, but we do not know what attracts us. It is still a mystery, but one with magical powers. We are drawn to what we do not understand. It is this mysterious meaningfulness which must be sought in terms of what we all are and what Hamlet is. A bond exists. So instinctively is it felt that it must transcend whatever secrets of the Tudor-Stuart age are known only to antiquarians. An immediate soul sympathy, if it is experienced by everyone quite irrespective of any intensive study in Shakespeare, we can begin to seek in those sacred areas of life which themselves bind different ages together.

The many roles in which we see Hamlet — prince, son, friend, lover, avenger, and something of a philosopher — are only the very rudimentary beginning. Hamlet is many things and would therefore appeal in a variety of ways — as opposed to some other fictional character who is essentially a lover or ruler. But before we can see through these roles into the one thing we must eventually find him to be — as indeed we must see through the sides to his character — they must be made clear. The parental theme is the first and most obvious of these. Hamlet's relationship to his parents is really quite simple and quite normal, though it has occasioned considerable discussion, both Freudian and non-Freudian, that seems destined to go on for many years to come. As it happens, thousands of characters from the pages of literature have been portrayed with no relationship to their parents, or with only a partial one. It little behooves us to wonder what was Claudio's attitude toward *his* mother, or Orsino's or Ferdinand's toward his. Obviously these men had mothers and, assuming a normal family life, loved them and would have reacted sharply to a second marriage similar to that of Gertrude's. But we know nothing of these and many other mothers, and where they do not exist there can be no filial love to occupy our attention. Even among the numerous cases in which a parent is portrayed the relationship is not important. The parents of both Romeo and Juliet, for instance, are decidedly minor characters, though perhaps memorable ones. Prince Henry, it is true, plays an important role as a son, but even here the question of Henry's princely duty is at least as important as any personal love he feels, or does not feel for his father. And while we can find portrayals of strong filial love, they invariably center around a tragic death or some other momentous event that would provoke tears and impassioned sentiments. It can be said, without exaggeration

I think, that in literature parents tend either to disappear entirely or to occupy a position of secondary importance. Hamlet's attitude toward his mother may therefore appear unusual, particularly in view of the fact that she has not been taken from him by death but is right there with him in an atmosphere of surrounding cordiality and normal everyday living. If we go this far, it is only a step to saying that Hamlet's love for his mother is abnormal and that Hamlet himself is eccentric, or even deranged.

What might be called the norms of literary subject matter, consequently, are likely to mislead the unwary literati who have become too engulfed in what "usually happens." T. S. Eliot, for instance, says that Hamlet's disgust with his mother is in excess of any conceivable cause that could explain it.[3] Hamlet's bafflement and inaction, according to Eliot, are simply the result of feelings that have no "objective correlative." Such a simple statement can hardly be its own proof. What the family means, certainly what the family *ought* to mean, cannot be so summarily dismissed. A simple examination of the facts and their relationship to the real world about us will easily show why.

For approximately two months Hamlet has mourned his father's death, a period of time which seems excessive to some others in the play (and perhaps to many readers). He is scarcely cheered by the King's philosophical reminder that sons have lost fathers from time immemorial and that we must all be prepared to accept such things, although many a reader finds the advice perfectly reasonable at the particular time in the play it is given, for we do not yet know that the one who gives it is the murderer, nor do we have the full appreciation just yet of the pain of Hamlet's loss. Enough is imparted, however, as to the recency of his father's death and as to his mother's second marriage that, even at this point, we have some glimmerings of why the King's adjurations increase rather than lessen his stepson's grief. What Claudius intends as comfort and strength to Hamlet is certainly not tactless or out of place. It is standard enough. But the dramatic moment at which Shakespeare first brings Hamlet before us is seldom fully grasped. Nor is it possible to grasp it just yet. In the light of the way this scene is developed, however, we may make a few pertinent observations. Regardless of how general death may be, the death experience is a poignantly individual one. It is precisely because death is so intensely individual that others do their utmost to share the sufferings of the bereaved, and by sharing lessen them. The efficacy of true sympathy is well recognized. I think anyone will grant my point. But — and here the reader must judge in the light of his own experiences, rather than as a dispassionate literary commentator — sympathy, however truly felt, can never be as intense or as enduring as the pain of the afflicted. Even when the death is a fictional one, the feelings of a surviving son can be conjectured at that point at which the unhappy event is presumed to be over: all mourners have departed and normal life has resumed, if it were ever seriously interrupted, among all his friends and companions, and he is left to himself with an ache that is more acute than ever. The finality of death strikes home, not while death is still recent, but only after the passage of weeks and months, and with the slow realization that a certain close one will never return.

It is at this precise moment that we first meet Hamlet. Claudius has declared that all mourning for the elder Hamlet is now finished, and the opening part of the scene is given over to the normal business of everyday life at court. Anyone who feels Hamlet's sorrow to be unduly prolonged and exaggerated is in the state of mind of one of Hamlet's sympathizers, not of Hamlet himself. Shakespeare deliberately introduces the Prince under circumstances that set forth the clash between his own feelings and what others think these feelings ought to be. Hamlet's sadness appears excessive because it is in fact in excess of that of others over the event which promoted it. This excess is the more striking as it leaves Hamlet to himself, since the rest of the world has returned to normalcy (though some of them ought not to). Hamlet's emotional reactions are very like what De Quincy discusses in his famous essay, "On the Knocking at the Gate in *Macbeth*," i.e., that the full impact of a dreadful crisis is felt, not so much during the suspension of normalcy during the crisis, but "at that moment when the suspension ceases, and the goings-on of human life are suddenly resumed." The reason for this in the case of Macbeth is that the utter realization of murder committed, is possible *only* when normal activity resumes and the murderer knows he cannot become normal with it; his crime brands him the more when he steps among the innocent and unknowing people about him.

Macbeth's sense of guilt can be likened to Hamlet's sorrow. Making allowances for the fact that bereavement is not crime and that in time a person may be expected to get over sorrow, we may still say that Macbeth and Hamlet come to their fullest realization of guilt and grief respectively when the difference between them and their fellows is at its widest. But where the emphasis of this disparity is prepared beforehand in *Macbeth*, it comes afterward in *Hamlet*. In the former play the horrible intensity of the murder scene is interrupted with the sharp crack of the knocking at the gate, followed by the comical porter scene. Normalcy has returned, but it can never be normalcy for Macbeth or for us who have followed the unspeakable horror in the criminal's mind and know of that murdered king lying in the room upstairs. Unless we know of these things in advance, the effect of the scene following is utterly lost.

In *Hamlet*, however, there is almost no prior conditioning of the audience to what the main character feels. The elder Hamlet's death is imparted in the opening scene, but not in such a way as to engender our sympathies for his family. It is mentioned by the King at the beginning of Scene ii, but briefly, and merely to tell us that mourning has been discontinued in the general festivities surrounding his and Gertrude's marriage. Hamlet is scarcely noticed as attention is then given to everyday matters of business, pleasure, affairs of state. The King speaks of the trouble with young Fortinbras and the mission of Voltimand and Cornelius to Norway, which latter, according to Claudius, is the main purpose of the present meeting. Next he turns his attention to the petition of Laertes, acquiesced in by Polonius, to return to France. We are engulfed in these other things to such an extent that we are far more in the mood of Claudius, Polonius, Laertes, and the others, than that of Hamlet. The fact that we have seen the ghost of the dead king in the previous scene does not alter this. That imported something dire; it told us nothing of the grief of the surviving son. Consequently, we tend to agree with the King when he calls Hamlet's persistent sorrow "unmanly grief." We are completely out of anything like true sympathy with Hamlet because we have not been permitted yet to enter into it. Shakespeare seems deliberately to put us into an indifferent frame of mind before admitting us into communion with Hamlet's sadness and permits the King to discourse at great length on the fact that losing a father is one of the commonest things in life.

Now, the object of this, as it was in *Macbeth,* is to make the audience appreciate the difference between the afflicted and the indifferent. Had we been sympathetic from the outset we might have appreciated the Prince's bereavement well enough. But we could never appreciate the added pain caused by the different states of mind of Hamlet and all these others in the King's court. The most effective way of achieving that is by putting us, the audience, into one frame of mind and then slowly working us into the other. It is not until all the others leave that we learn the true state of Hamlet's mind as he bursts forth in his bitter soliloquy:

> Oh, that this too too solid flesh would melt,
> Thaw, and resolve itself into a dew!
> Or that the Everlasting had not fixed

His canon 'gainst self-slaughter! Oh, God! God!
How weary, stale, flat, and unprofitable
Seem to me all the uses of this world!
Fie on't, ah, fie! 'Tis an unweeded garden,
That grows to seed, things rank and gross in nature
Possess it merely. That it should come to this!
But two months dead! Nay, not so much, not two.
So excellent a King, that was, to this,
Hyperion to a satyr. So loving to my mother
That he might not beteem the winds of heaven
Visit her face too roughly. Heaven and earth!
Must I remember? Why, she would hang on him
As if increase of appetite had grown
By what it fed on. And yet within a month —
Let me not think on't. — Fraility, thy name is woman! —

Not only does this sharp reversal of mood convey to us
how sad and bitter Hamlet is, not only does it accentuate
the difference between him and the others, but it tells us
things of which we may have had only an imperfect realization when they were mentioned earlier in the scene.
Had Shakespeare presented those around Hamlet as nor-
mally sympathetic over the death of his father—particularly the King and Queen who are brother and wife, after
all — Hamlet's sorrow would not be so marked, since it
would not be so at variance with that of the rest of the
court. As it is, the contrast is intended to work at first in
Hamlet's disfavor with the audience, but if this disfavor
persists, it is through failure to follow a dramatic pro-
gression from a covering gloss to a hidden sorrow.

Early as this soliloquy occurs in the play, it should be
read only after careful consideration of what has taken
place prior to it. The opening scene is at night, heavy
with the atmosphere of darkness and a mysterious ghost
that appears twice on the ramparts without speaking. It
is a grim scene and a black one, preparing us for the
sharp contrast of rich color with which the second scene
opens. That this scene does open with a panoply of color
is obvious from the discussion as to why "the clouds still
hang on" Hamlet. No one else is dressed in mourning

weeds. On the contrary, the gowns and robes of the ladies and gentlemen of the court, the royal ermine and the flashing jewelry of the kingly crown all create a blazing array of finery. Yet the memory of that ominous ghost is kept alive as the blackness of that first scene narrows to one small portion of the stage: Hamlet himself. The remarkable symbolism of his "nighted color" establishes a link with another being that broods over Denmark with secrets fearful and unspoken. That Hamlet is out of step with the brilliant assemblage is unimportant in itself, nor can he be deemed right or wrong thereby. He is mysteriously designated to play quite another role, one that is in no way to be judged by his conformity to the society in which we find him. He will be responsible, not to that society, but to a spirit beyond it. And that spirit will say nothing contrary to Hamlet's vituperations in this first soliloquy.

That Hamlet does not know of the murder at this juncture is beside the point. He blames no one for his father's death. He is, however, aware of something very unnatural in the unseemly marriage between his mother and Claudius, and the bitter grief over his father's death gives him a clearer vision of that marriage than any of the indifferent members of court can possibly have. And while it is true that neither he nor we yet know of the murder, Hamlet's "It is not, nor it cannot, come to good" shows a perception which succeeding events thoroughly justify. Not a perception of secrets as yet unrevealed, but the perception of a soul in love with the beauty of the Christian ideal. If, from all indications in the play, we try to reconstruct the perfect love that must once have united Hamlet and his parents, we are led to envision a sinless union: father, mother and son enveloped in a love of perfect harmony.

That Hamlet could find in the remembrance of this union sufficient reason for feeling so strongly against his mother now is, of course, perfectly conceivable. We are not at all concerned with whether such family concord is the normal thing (particularly in our own day), so long as we can say that it does sometimes happen and that it is an ideal which, once experienced, would provoke an extreme bitterness if it were lost. Even those who never possessed it need not necessarily be without some appreciation of its beauty; certainly Shakespeare's age had the perfect example of the Holy Family brought continually before it. How much this ideal has been lost since is difficult to say, but the reaction of later ages to the melancholy prince who has also lost it may be well worth pondering.

It is not the least bit surprising, therefore, that while the cause of Hamlet's grief is his father's death, this first revelation of his feelings is almost wholly concerned with his mother's marriage. The first event ended Hamlet's perfect world, but the second one violated it. Grief Hamlet might have endured silently and passively, but what he felt to be slime cast upon a pure white memory could never be accepted so. His thoughts should take no one unaware, as a paradoxical revelation of the subconscious might be presumed to do, if he really identified himself with his father and was therefore jealous of his mother's loving someone else. Tidy formulas like this are nothing but clumsy attempts to fill the gap of rejected morality. For if we discard the notion that Hamlet's feelings have a moral basis, we have to substitute something or they go unexplained altogether. It is really the vehemence of these feelings that perplexes modern critics, who think that Hamlet should have reacted in a more demure way. But surely the scathing bitterness with which the ghost denounces Gertrude puts the condemnation of her action quite beyond any merely personal motivation. In fact, this second marriage of hers is conspicuously unaccountable until the ghost enlightens us. Adultery and murder precede it. Evil as these crimes are, they impart a certain logic or consistency to this strange queen who followed the dead body of her first husband "like Niobe all tears." But while the ghost's revelation may answer Hamlet's burning question, it confirms, in the very worst way possible, whatever suspicions the question may tend to formulate. Hamlet becomes satisfied intellectually, but only at the expense of a greater moral shock. His later passivity is due in part to his complete knowledge. With the emergence of facts he must accept and live with, the hot interest of a dreadful curiosity dies away. But we are anticipating a little too much at the moment.

To explain any of these things by delving into the esoteric, while it has the attraction of escaping the plebeian and the obvious, will miss the point of Hamlet's character and the entire purpose of the play. While the play does concern itself with involved and inexpressible realities, these are lost utterly if we have taken the wrong approach at the beginning. The temptation to employ abstruse terms must be resisted, even at the cost of falling occasionally into platitudes. The less conventional we make Hamlet the narrower his appeal becomes — at least theoretically — but in reality it is difficult to name a fictional character with a broader appeal. The fact is that we first meet Hamlet in the throes of a sorrow all men can readily understand, and we see him abandoned in that sorrow as all of us — though to a considerably lesser extent — have also been abandoned. In our quest for the generic or universal we hit upon a profound, though by no means unusual, fact: Hamlet is an idealist disillusioned. Our first view of him is that of a youth with an acute sense of paradise lost, or of an ideal world that has ceased to be. The first words he expresses when he is alone show a desire for death because life is too "weary, stale, flat, and unprofitable." Things rank and gross in nature possess it. It is an unweeded garden. This desire for death, which he repeats later in the play, is the result of his not being able to face the world now that he has found out what it is really like. But why not?

Abundant evidence, both direct and indirect, refutes the notion that the young prince has led a particularly sheltered life. As a student at the university and as the scholar and soldier described by Ophelia, he has had interests and experiences apart from family life, so that we can hardly think that his parents have been his "world" up to now. The belief in an ideal need not be predicated on ignorance of all else, and while it is not improbable that Hamlet has learned something about life, the educational aspect is the least important one. When he speaks of the world as being entirely bad and frailty as synonymous with woman, though he may be wrong in his facts, he is undoubtedly maturing under the impact of a terrible blow. What is more to the point, however, is the light focused through his bitterness on the thing lost. This desecrated purity, unimpressive as an abstraction, turns to glittering reality as we perceive it with Hamlet's eyes — the more it recedes from him and from us the more do we strain after it. As that light fades, the ordinary light of the world he now inhabits must seem like darkness.

The powerful turmoil in Hamlet's mind may seem excessive to many people, but only if they confine their speculations to Hamlet. The ghost cannot be dismissed so easily, nor can Gertrude's admission when her son confronts her with what she has done. It is clear that Shakespeare intended Hamlet's view to be interrupted as . . . I recoil from using words like "correct" or "proper" because, while not exactly out of place, they suggest a calculated pronouncement quite unlike the passionate intensity of the soliloquy. Rather than assume an ordinary situation that could not justify Hamlet's overpowering sense of loss, we ought more logically to assume a state of near perfection. Either way we must work by inferences. But Hamlet, a man of reasonably cosmopolitan experience and mature judgment, is himself a strong argument for us to assume the latter. With this question, as with most things in life itself, categorical negatives are more difficult to prove than categorical affirmatives. I could give much more evidence to support the sweeping statement that every man's mother has meant essentially the same thing to him that Gertrude once meant to Hamlet—more, I say, than anyone could give to prove that no man's mother could possibly mean that much. There is no need, however, to choose between arbitrary generalizations. All we need insist upon is that it is *possible* for Gertrude to have once been such an ideal wife and mother as to scandalize her son to the extent she does by an open faithlessness to her husband. If that much can be granted, it would not be amiss to measure Hamlet's affection against millions of filial relationships in all times and places. I believe the results would be far closer to the categorial affirmative, even in those ages in which the family has fallen from the elevated position it held in the day of Shakespeare.

Hamlet is an idealist. While this word has been used to designate many different things — visionary, reformer, perfectionist, blind optimist — I think for the sake of argument we can restrict it to one of two possible meanings: the man who believes that perfection can be achieved in life, or the man who expects perfection to be already there. We may broaden the term "perfection" to include "as near perfection as humanly possible," since many an idealist realizes the impossibility of achieving the absolute. Now, there is quite a difference between these two types. The first, the one who believes perfection can be achieved, must be a man of action and never-flagging confidence. He must be a realist who, despite the perfection he dreams of, has no illusions about the way things are. He must have a clear view of the world as it is and an equally clear view of what he hopes it can be made into. He must not be easily discouraged, he must not expect immediate results; if he does, his vision is not so clear as it ought to be and he is more like the second type than the first. We cannot say that this second type "must be" or "must not be" anything. He simply is or he is not. Nor does he require any special explanation. He is as much the idealist as is the first, but with the decided difference that he is descending from a once-envisioned perfection whereas the other is mounting toward it. The man who believes the world perfect as it is is in for sore disappointment sooner or later, and is in danger of turning cynical or afraid or both.

It can easily be seen what kind of idealist Hamlet is. He is in no sense a reformer. His view of an ideal past (which can be inferred from his view of a corrupted present), his cynicism, his desire for death all mark him as the latter of the two types I have described. Furthermore, he is too concerned with himself in the first place — *his* sufferings, *his* troubles, *his* cares, and later *his* failure to act — ever to do much thinking of bettering others. Even when he generalizes he is speaking of himself or things that affect himself. When he calls the world "an unweeded garden," he is speaking of a world more deeply entrenched in his heart than any other. "Frailty, thy name is woman!" may indeed be meant to apply to all women, but it is said only on account of his mother and what she has done. Even later when Hamlet soliloquizes on man's inhumanity to man, the point is missed entirely if he is thought to be evincing a real concern for the sufferings of others. He makes sweeping statements because his own pain is so intense and so horribly real. A man bitterly disappointed in love is quick to think all women false. Or a man who discovers falsity in a trusted friend will easily think the whole world untrustworthy. Right or wrong, he will think and speak far beyond the bounds of his own experience because the intensity of his own pain is more powerfully convincing than years of calculated observation would be.

That such a person exaggerates we need hardly be told. We are perfectly correct when we think Hamlet unreasonable in saying all women are frail simply because his own mother is, but such an objective conclusion should not omit some insight into the state of mind which indulges in such broad generalizations. We must judge Hamlet sympathetically and realize that his suffering usurps his heart, his vision, his logic, his very philosophy of life. A man in agony speaks loud and large because he must. He must condemn in an all-inclusive way because his own entire being is stricken. Unless he have the poet's articulateness which enables him to speak of his own suffering in words sufficiently meaningful to express all he feels, he must make up in numbers what he cannot achieve in severity. His conclusions are illogical because they are statements rather than questions. That is, he is sullenly positive now as he was blithely sure in the past. The harsh revelation that he was wrong has not caused him to wonder, but to be just as sure of the opposite extreme. He was once certain the world was white. Now he is just as certain it is black. This conviction is feelingly stated in two of the four soliloquies, but each time it is quickly followed by the deterring notion of the "canons 'gainst self-slaughter" and the "something after death" which blocks the thought of self-annihilation. Such thoughts are not very happy ones as far as they go. They argue very powerfully for a life of much disappointment and frustration, and only two possible solutions offer themselves: either the conviction that life *can* be made happy and rewarding, or the belief in life after death as the ultimate goal and fulfilment of our desires. We have already seen that Hamlet is no reformer, and we can easily see that he does not do enough thinking about the afterlife to derive much comfort from it. He acknowledges it in terms unmistakable and there is no doubt that it serves as a guide to his conduct by way of prohibition, but that is as far as he goes. The only alternative left to him is to turn back to the first. Yet, in doing this Hamlet would seem to bound back again and yearn for something like an other-worldly existence:

> What a piece of work is man! How noble in reason! How
> infinite in faculty! In form and moving how express and
> admirable! In action how like an angel! In apprehension how
> like a god! The beauty of the world! The paragon of animals!

Can a creature so vast feel anything but cramped in the mass of petty circumstances and severe disappointments that make up so much of this life? On the other hand this passage is not what we would call mystical or religiously spiritual. It is a noble description of the nature of man, but more conscious of the fact that man belongs *out* of this world than that he belongs *in* any other. It is a more open expression of the idealistic Hamlet than can be immediately detected in the first soliloquy, but both speeches are characterized by dissatisfaction with this life rather than satisfaction with some future one. It is not that he disbelieves in the future life; his words indicate that he does believe in it. But whether his faith is not strong enough or because of some other inadequacy on his part, the fact remains that he is preoccupied with the present existence and its attendant ills. In this state of mind he is afflicted with a series of further reversals and overwhelming conclusions as to the sordidness that lies all about him. Within a short time his love for Ophelia, a love we have every reason to believe sincere, is doomed. His friends Rosencrantz and Guildenstern do not measure up to what might be expected of sincere friendship. Most important of all is the terrible and difficult duty enjoined upon him by the ghost of his dead father.

That Hamlet has been deprived of the throne is a question scholars have debated, the point at issue being whether he would succeed by election or by virtue of his royal descent. Without attempting to rule on this, we may certainly conclude that the Prince has ample reason for doubting the assurance of the murderer Claudius that he stands next in line. Hamlet continually speaks of himself as possessing nothing:

> . . . to speak to you like an honest man,
> I am most dreadfully attended.
> Beggar that I am . . .
> I eat the air, promise-crammed.

And in avenging his father upon the present King, Hamlet would remove all possibility of Claudius's promise carrying any weight, as well as jeopardizing his own claim to the throne and personal safety as well.

To return to the universality of *Hamlet*. The picture with which we are presented at the outset is a far from pleasant one, nor will it become any more pleasant as the play proceeds. The disappointment in Ophelia's love, in the friendship of Rosencrantz and Guildenstern, the duty to which Hamlet will have to devote himself, these all develop as the play unfolds, and they serve to intensify the unhappiness of these first few scenes. To see a universal appeal or a wide applicability in a work so progressively unhappy would seem to presuppose a very pessimistic view of creation on the part of many people. Perhaps it would, but if such be the case it is the result of an imperfect awareness of what all great tragedy means. The sordidness of what is wrong depends upon the sacredness of what is right. A tragedy must imply that, or it is no tragedy. Hamlet's feelings about his father, his mother, and his uncle-stepfather fill him with sadness and with loathing. What does this do but point up the beauty of parental relationship when it is ideal? The same is true of his ill-fated love for Ophelia. If we overlook the idealism Hamlet expected to find in each case, we miss the devastating effect upon him of the corrupt and the commonplace. But we do more than this. We manufacture a curious contradiction in which we are obliged to explain what appeals in terms of what depresses and revolts us. The paradox can be resolved only if we follow it through to its logical implications. Gertrude's actions deserve condemnation in themselves, but they enhance rather than detract from the role of motherhood and the solemnity of the marriage vow. The memory of the elder Hamlet's virtues is kept ever fresh by the vices of Claudius who usurped his place. Perfection, even by its absence, is conspicuous throughout, and it is the essential beauty of this theme that those who love the play instinctively feel. Logically enough, it is those who would condone Gertrude and Claudius in an amoralistic attempt to gloss over the ugliness Hamlet is forced to face — and thereby condemn his mission of justice as a false code of honor — who miss this beauty altogether.

Of the various units which comprise the total set of relationships in which we discover Hamlet, I have treated the parental one in some detail in this opening chapter for two reasons: first because it is the first one indicated in the play, and second because I wish to dispel at the outset the notion that Hamlet is the victim of a mental aberration of any kind. His feeling for his mother and father have, more than anything else, given rise to this idea, and if we permit ourselves to read the remainder of the play with this fixed in our minds it may easily lead us to conclusions with which many later developments cannot be reconciled. Strange as the Prince's character may be, men have ever felt that immediate response to him which does not bear out any supposed abnormalcy, or *untypical-ness*, unless we are all abnormal ourselves. This is said before entering into any detailed study of his character because I realize that, while what *happens* to Hamlet may be representative in its way, his reaction to what happens may be regarded as unique. With respect to this reaction there is nothing strange or unusual except for the fact that Hamlet appears to be a highly sensitive youth, one who feels a hurt deeply and lastingly. But sensitivity is not abnormalcy. It is merely an intensification of normalcy. The only alternative to sensitivity is indifference, and if we agree that only the inanimate can be completely indifferent and have no reaction whatever to the things about it, sensitivity of some kind may be taken as quite normal in human beings.

The question is, how much? When it passes beyond a certain point, resultant behavior may become unreasonable and abnormal even though the difference be one of degree rather than kind. Understand that it is a difference of *degree,* not of *kind.* Even a very powerful affection on the part of Hamlet for his mother need not indicate an unnatural affection. Attraction does not become perverse because it is strong, any more than it is normal because it is weak. Nor need his repugnance to his mother's disaffection from the tears she shed at the death of the elder Hamlet be taken as in any way the result of a twisted or unnatural disappointment. Hamlet's sensitivity in this is not unnatural, but part of the above question remains: it is unduly strong? This answers itself when we remember the time element. The "within a month" period during which Gertrude buries one husband whom "she would hang on...as if increase of appetite had grown by what it fed on," whose dead body she followed "like Niobe all tears" — and her taking a second husband, constitutes a pattern of behavior that forces the very reaction we see in Hamlet and precludes any other.

One fact, however, seems to indicate otherwise. Hamlet is all by himself in his feelings and completely out of step with the rest of the court. I believe that this persuades our own age particularly that Hamlet is to some degree unusual. The Prince is, be it admitted, maladjusted. He does not fit into the society in which he lives, and if we are in the habit of thinking that maladjustment is wrong absolutely, and not merely inconvenient, we are obliged to find Hamlet wrong on this point alone. This question involves many things too large for me to get into here, but the fact remains that maladjustment is never wrong *per se*, but only when it involves culpable acts that can definitely be pinpointed. Society is not always right, and though Hamlet may be guilty as charged we can infer nothing from it but that he believes one way and the world about him apparently believes another. The general assent to the marriage of Gertrude and Claudius can no more make it right than a crime wave in modern society could make burglary morally better on the ground that more people are committing it. The facts of the play require that we judge every character by a fixed set of values; we cannot do this by going into moral oblivion and coming up with the sterile conclusion that Hamlet is a statistical oddity.

In real life such a problem offers no easy solutions as long as we recognize a natural difference between the poignancy of one's private feelings and the apathy of the many. It is idle to think the two can ever be perfectly reconciled, though under more favorable circumstances they can be brought closer together. This is what we ought to mean by *adjustment* as opposed to *maladjustment,* but it can exist only under ideal conditions in which adjustment does not entail any bargaining with evil. There is no question about the guilt of Gertrude and Claudius, as the story amply demonstrates. Hamlet is informed of all by the ghost, the Queen bares her guilt-ridden conscience to Hamlet, and Claudius admits his chief crime to himself on two separate occasions.

Thus Shakespeare introduces us to his hero in a way that combines several important considerations. From the outset his painful loss reflects, to a greater or lesser extent, a common experience of mankind. It need not be specifically the loss of a father, though that in itself would be common enough. Hamlet is perfectly normal in his reaction to it. And in this reaction he is removed from society and must suffer by himself, for the world cannot or will not suffer with him. As the play unfolds we get a deeper picture of him, involving sides to his character which augment even where they seem to contradict what we find at the outset. He cannot be justified in everything he does, nor is it easy to condemn him. But he can always be reconciled with what we have first found him to be.

One thing more. In no other Shakespearian character is there the sympathy between audience and character that there is in the play *Hamlet.* In other plays this dramatic sympathy comes only now and then, and invariably it is divided among several characters. Exceptions to this, such as the Richard plays, involve action which is restricted in appeal — as it is in *King Lear* — and which is of a somewhat unusual quality. But in the play we are considering, the communion between the audience and the central character is so thorough that the other characters, however exhaustively portrayed, are seen as outsiders. We see them, even when Hamlet is absent, with him uppermost in our thoughts.

I again use the term *sympathy* in the sense that De Quincey uses it in the essay already alluded to, "a sympathy of comprehension, a sympathy by which we enter into his feelings, and are made to understand them — not a sympathy of pity or approbation ... " We enter into the feelings of Hamlet and understand them more than anyone else in the play does, with the possible exception of Horatio. Mainly through the soliloquies we read Hamlet's thoughts and all his actions in a way impossible to the other characters. The revelation of the murder and the duty of avenging it are imparted to Hamlet and to us at the same time, but to no one else. That Horatio knows about it later is very clearly indicated when Hamlet tells him to watch his uncle during the performance of the play, and refers to having told him of the circumstances of his father's death. But this is long afterward, and since we do not see Hamlet revealing the secret to his friend nor do we ever learn precisely how much he reveals, it cannot lessen our consciousness of its weight on Hamlet. Horatio's sharing the perilous confidence can do almost nothing to impart dramatic sympathy to two characters instead of one. The load of suffering and unfulfilled duty is, to all intents and purposes, Hamlet's burden and ours. We learn all his sorrows and disappointments from Hamlet himself. Others in the play, if they mention these things at all, mention them in the most unsympathetic way and with almost no appreciation of their importance to Hamlet. Shakespeare studiously avoids any presentation of the Prince's afflictions and dread duty except through the mind of Hamlet himself. This is not necessarily Shakespeare's way. *The Winter's Tale* opens with a conversation between Camillo and Archidamus who reveal an acute awareness of the deep friendship between Leontes and Polixenes. One of the most moving passages in *Richard II* is York's description of the pathetic Richard riding through the streets behind his conqueror Bolingbroke. In *The Merchant of Venice*, the friendship of Antonio and Bassanio is nowhere so affectingly described as in Salarino's telling of their taking leave of each other. Many more instances could be offered in which others have a vivid realization of the innermost feelings, be they happy or sad, of an important character.

Now, while this further explains the appeal of Hamlet and offers additional evidence of his separation from those around him, we are still a long way from what we are seeking to find. Hamlet has to *be* something that appeals; he can never be this something, whatever it is, out of a mere intimacy of delineation plus the fact that his problems are ours. It is true that the dramatic sympathy by which Shakespeare presents and enlarges his character is the medium especially chosen and perfectly suited to a character in which men may see themselves. Whereever there is this dramatic sympathy in the portrayal of a character, there is bound to be an intimacy between him and the audience. But with most characters this is largely an intimacy of knowledge, not of self-identification. Hamlet remains unique along all such portrayals. Knowledge of his character continues to be something of a mystery, but that indefinable something else that makes Hamlet you and you Hamlet grows stronger than ever. Who can explain it? I believe we can go a long way toward explaining it by seeing all things and characters and Hamlet himself in proper perspective and proper sequence, but at the end of it all Hamlet will remain a mystery — not as completely a mystery as he now is to many, but as much so as the man in all times and places whom Prince Hamlet represents.

II

THE SENSE
OF DUTY

Since the duty of avenging his father's murder is the next thing revealed to us in connection with Hamlet I will discuss that at length before continuing with the Prince in relation to his various roles, or functions. Most of his relationship to these is seen only after we find him laboring under this sense of duty. It vitally affects all he says and does and we must be clear about one if we are to be correct about the other.

Let us eliminate much that might be said of Hamlet's reaction to the terrible news that his father was murdered, and Claudius the murderer. What concerns us most is Hamlet's strange inconsistency directly afterward. This inconsistency has been pointed out so often that it is as well known, possibly, as any one of the major soliloquies. For the sake of completeness I would like to include it here, since it is the first indication we have of the most puzzling side to Hamlet's character: the long delay in avenging his father's death, even though he seems to have every motive for going ahead with it. Compare Hamlet's first reaction to the news just after the ghost vanishes, with what he says at the close of the same scene:

> O all you host of Heaven! O earth! What else?
> And shall I couple Hell? Oh, fie! Hold, hold, my heart,
> And you, my sinews, grow not instant old
> But bear me stiffly up. Remember thee!
> Aye, thou poor ghost, while memory holds a seat
> In this distracted globe. Remember thee!
> Yea, from the table of my memory
> I'll wipe away all trivial fond records,
> All saws of books, all forms, all pressures past,
> That youth and observation copied there,
> And thy commandment all alone shall live
> Within the book and volume of my brain,
> Unmixed with baser matter. Yes, by Heaven!
> O most pernicious woman!
> O villain, villain, smiling, damned villain!
> My tables — meet it is I set it down
> (*Writing*) That one may smile, and smile, and be a villain.
> At least I'm sure it may be so in Denmark.
> So, Uncle, there you are. Now to my word.
> It is "Adieu, adieu! Remember me."
> I have sworn't.

Yet, after a short time elapses during which he has been speaking with Horatio and Marcellus, he says this:

> The time is out of joint. Oh, cursed spite
> That ever I was born to set it right!

This falling off of determination characterizes Hamlet in the pursuit of his mission throughout the remainder of the action, and although the play has been called the tragedy of a man who cannot make up his mind, the plain

place over a period of time for it to suggest itself to Polonius as a likely explanation for Hamlet's "madness." Polonius then goes to the King and Queen with this explanation, but before he gives it, in the following scene, the royal pair conducts two audiences. The first is with Rosencrantz and Guildenstern, Hamlet's two close friends, who have been "sent for." Whatever passage of time may be deduced from this fact would have to allow some period for strange behavior on the part of Prince Hamlet, long enough for the King and Queen to have known and worried about it sufficiently to send for Rosencrantz and Guildenstern; a messenger's journey to them and their journey to Elsinore would have come on top of this.

We who study the play *Hamlet* are often accused of scrutinizing too closely the text of something written for live performance on the boards. We may at times "consider too curiously to consider so," but the reason lies partially in the fact that our modern age of jet propulsion renders contemporary audiences a tiny bit oblivious to what was crystal clear to Elizabethans. To them a journey of any length meant the passage of weeks, sometimes months. When, in the same scene we are considering, Voltimand and Cornelius return from Norway, to which place they started in Act I, an Elizabethan theatre goer would have assumed immediately what has often to be pointed out to us: considerable time has passed in the interim. He would not have had to rely on Ophelia's remark to point it out to him, nor should we if we follow developments with any kind of attention. Incident after incident through Act II piles up the evidence that time has gone by, and this following on the heels of Hamlet's change of heart at the conclusion of Act I, is enough to make us begin to wonder. When Hamlet does finally appear in this sequence, he is reading a book. The significance of this is too often lost sight of because of the attention given to Hamlet's insanity and the little "mad" act which he puts on at this point. The mere appearance of Hamlet absorbed in his reading instead of thinking about what his father's ghost had charged him to do, is the first conclusive indication of what he himself elaborates upon in the passionate soliloquy which closes the scene. Even though this reading is interrupted by Polonius and again by Rosencrantz and Guildenstern, it is not until after the arrival of the players that Hamlet is recalled to his path of duty.

When the players arrive Hamlet requests one of them to recite a speech he remembers the player to have given once before. The player complies with the Prince's request and forces himself into a show of emotion so convincing as to appear almost real — tears, broken voice, gesture, and facial expression suiting perfectly the lines he speaks, as if it were not all a fiction but an actual experience about which the actor is talking. The effect on Hamlet is devastating. All the time he has been watching and listening to this realistic portrayal of what true grief is, he becomes slowly aware of the indifference of which he has himself been guilty. He cannot help contrasting the actor's performance with his own utter lack of feeling, he who has every reason for exhibiting emotion:

> What would he do
> Had he the motive and the cue for passion
> That I have? He would drown the stage with tears
> . . .
> Yet I,
> A dull and muddy-mettled rascal, peak,
> Like John-a-dreams, unpregnant of my cause,
> And can say nothing — no, not for a King
> Upon whose property and most dear life
> A damned defeat was made.

It is not the problem of what to do, but the appalling clarity of it that explodes upon Hamlet with the force of a thunderclap. Not only is his duty painfully clear to him, not only is his failure to pursue it equally so, but he speaks all in words unmistakeable and with no attempt to soften what he conceives to be his contemptible lack of action. Why has he not acted?

                    Am I a coward?
Who calls me villain? Breaks my pate across?
Plucks off my beard and blows it in my face?
Tweaks me by the nose? Gives me the lie i' the throat
As deep as to the lungs? Who does me this?
Ha!
'Swounds, I should take it. For it cannot be
But I am pigeon-livered and lack gall
To make oppression bitter, or ere this
I should have fatted all the region kites
With this slave's offal.

Some commentators have said that Hamlet is compelled to inaction by one of the most important things he must accomplish before taking any definite steps: securing proof positive that the King *is* guilty, rather than rely upon the word of the ghost. It is maintained that the arrival of the players at Elsinore suggests to Hamlet a means of accomplishing this which he would not otherwise have had, and that once his course of action is determined he proceeds upon his way. It is, perhaps, a little difficult to imagine what Hamlet might have done had the players never arrived, furnishing the means as well as the idea. But we cannot say that Hamlet was waiting for just such an opportunity to present itself. The very force of the soliloquy here is not one of thankfulness that at last the means have been given him of going ahead, but rather an agonized realization that he has not thought about it at all, or at least he has not been preoccupied with it to the extent that some positive action on his part might have already been accomplished. His words clearly state that he should have "fatted all the region kites with this slave's offal" long before this, and if we still insist he could not have done it, having had no opportunity, the fact remains that he has not even been seeking one.

Nevertheless, Hamlet, recalled now to a sense of duty, goes through with his plans for the play which will reënact the murder before the guilty King's eyes.

                              If he but blench,
I know my course.

The play works to perfection. The King rises and hurries from the room; the performance ends in confusion and everyone else leaves, except Hamlet and Horatio who compare notes. The King is guilty. All the certainty Hamlet has been in need of he now has. His path lies clear before him. But, what according to some commentators is highly important, the King knows that Hamlet knows. He is going to be doubly dangerous to deal with and Hamlet must proceed with infinite caution — if indeed he can proceed at all — because the King can be expected, not only to take measures to safeguard himself, but to seek the life of the Prince who is in on the grim secret. Hamlet has made progress but is also in actual danger and must remain constantly alive to the fact. All this may be true enough, but it cannot adequately explain Hamlet's failure to follow up his advantage and resort to some kind of definite action. The passage of time from the point after the play to catch the conscience of the King is perhaps more vaguely indicated than it was prior to the play, but that it passes and Hamlet is still "lapsed in time and passion," is certainly clear from the final soliloquy. Just as his self-reproach after listening to the impassioned speech of the actor would be pointless if he had in any way been thwarted by external circumstances, so it would be equally as pointless in the next instance. He chances to see an army of soldiers on their way to risk their lives for a small patch of disputed ground that could actually mean very little to any of them except that there is honor in fighting for it. The soliloquy he delivers on this occasion stresses the unflattering comparison between his attitude toward his duty and the attitude of others toward theirs. "How all occasions do inform against me and spur my dull revenge!" he exclaims; and, "Examples gross as earth exhort me." He speaks of the example immediately before him:

> Witness this army, of such mass and charge,
> Led by a delicate and tender Prince
> Whose spirit with divine ambition puffed

> Makes mouths at the invisible event,
> Exposing what is mortal and unsure
> To all that fortune, death, and danger dare,
> Even for an eggshell. Rightly to be great
> Is not to stir without great argument,
> But greatly to find quarrel in a straw
> When honor's at the stake.

He compares their conduct with the example he himself has given:

> How stand I then,
> That have a father killed, a mother stained,
> Excitements of my reason and my blood,
> And let all sleep while to my shame I see
> The imminent death of twenty thousand men
> That for a fantasy and trick of fame
> Go to their graves like beds, fight for a plot
> Whereon the numbers cannot try the cause,
> Which is not tomb enough and continent
> To hide the slain?

Hamlet's conduct is inexplicable, even to himself. His failure is right there before him, horribly and unavoidably there, but what name to give to it is a puzzle to him and has been to many a scholar.

> Now whether it be
> Bestial oblivion, or some craven scruple
> Of thinking too precisely on the event —
> A thought which, quartered, hath but one part wisdom
> And ever three parts coward — I do not know
> Why yet I live to say "This thing's to do,"
> Sith I have cause, and will, and strength, and means
> To do 't.

The line "thinking too precisely on the event," may be interpreted by some to mean planning and planning without ever doing, thinking out how to proceed — to such an extent that no procedure is ever forthcoming. How, it may be asked, can a person "think too precisely on the event" and not think of it at all? Isn't this an indication that Hamlet *has* been trying to think of a way to proceed but that the difficulty of the King's now knowing Hamlet is in on the guilty secret makes it impossible for the Prince to hit upon a plan that has any likelihood of success?

First of all, I do not maintain that Hamlet has not been thinking about it *in this second instance.* I say he was not thinking about it up to the time the player unwittingly called it to his mind, or if he were it was not with the burning desire he ought to have felt. Now we can allow that, after the King has revealed his guilt, Hamlet has at least been thinking of what he ought to do, since he tells us so himself, but it can hardly be that this "thinking too precisely on the event" implies any constructive plans for action. I might be tempted to think so if there were the slightest hint anywhere else that that is what he had been doing; but since there is not and since he plainly says, "Oh, from this time forth, My thoughts be bloody or be nothing worth!" we can hardly conclude that, whatever mental deliberations he may have undergone and however they were concerned with "the event," they consisted of practical plans as to how to bring it about. If he makes the resolution that his thoughts are to be bloody from this time forth, it is safe to assume they have not been so up to now. The pointed self-reproach of the entire soliloquy tells us this.

Rather this "thinking too precisely" is the fascination of dread, of repulsion from doing what is inescapable. It is what we mean today when we say of a person that he has something "on his mind." It may be worry, it may be trepidation, it may be a desire to escape the ordeal; whatever it is, it is a load and not a driving force. It is the state of mind of one trying to get up nerve enough to dive from a high board. The longer he stands there and thinks about it the more difficult it becomes. His mind is wholly bent upon what he wants to do, not on the way to do it. He is probably thinking of what will actually take place, a dread fascination of the reality of doing, in which case the word "event" can be taken in its literal sense, and which the lines, "A thought which, quartered, hath but one part wisdom and ever three parts coward," fit perfectly.

Now, if there is one noteworthy thing which characterizes Hamlet in both of these instances it is the honesty
of mind with which he views his failure to act. He does
not excuse or pretend or falsify in any way. On the contrary, he speaks with scorching plainness about his apparent lack of courage. Never does he paint it in any but
the worst light. His assignment is a difficult and perilous
one, but although he must be aware of the difficulty and
the danger he does not offer these as excuses. He has
accepted the task, as he inevitably must, and still wonders
at his reluctance to grapple with it. The terrible question
burns its way into his brain: Is it cowardice?

We who study the character of the Prince should be
as honest with him as he is with himself. We should see
him in a sympathetic and charitable light without attempting to eliminate what we do not like to find. Those who
insist that Hamlet never gets a chance to kill the King
attempt this. They try to explain away something that
they feel renders contemptible an otherwise truly lovable
and sympathetic character, forgetting as they do that
Hamlet himself never says a word about having had no
chance to act. He takes no refuge in this supposed lack
of opportunity (even if his admirers do), but condemns
himself in the most opprobrious terms. His duty and his
failure to do it are both unpalatably clear to him, not comfortably vague, and as Hamlet examines his own heart he
cannot find a shred of the many excuses that scholars
have found for him. He does not alter his own views of
himself by the slightest bit of coloration in order to render himself less ignominious in his own eyes. He does not
point to other brave things he has done to furnish an answer to his question, "Am I a coward?" He is concerned
exclusively with his present weakness and is not in the
least tempted to raise himself by virtue of his having
shown courage on other occasions.

This I find the most noble thing about the character
of Hamlet. He takes an honest view of his own weakness.
Men delight in portraying their weaknesses in a heroic

and attractive light either by processes of selection or addition or slight variation, so that we see weakness, not for what it actually is, but for something different, be it altered ever so slightly. This tendency is also there when men are considering someone they like or admire. Weakness must be seen in some agreeable way lest it sully the attractions that exist in spite of it. The most obvious method of accomplishing this is to find some reason for it that will render it perfectly sound and logical. "Caesar never did wrong without just cause" seems to be the unconscious attitude of many toward Hamlet. "Why does Hamlet delay as long as he does?" is the question continually asked, the clear implication being that there must be a reason and that it must be a satisfactory one. Those who hold that the Prince was a coward are quite willing to admit there is no reason, no *adequate* reason, why the killing of the King could not have been accomplished much sooner. But I must ask why Hamlet attracts such sympathetic response from so many people if all he is is a coward? What both sides forget — those who would excuse and those who would condemn — is that Hamlet's failure cannot be defended, but his truthful attitude toward that failure can be. Not only can it be defended, but the very humility of it exalts him to the realm of the truly saintly. It is not the convenient acknowledgment made by the coward who has no intention of ever being brave. Falstaff frankly prefers being a live coward to being a dead hero. But no one can pretend that Hamlet, who has even gone so far as to wish he had never been born to receive the duty that devolves upon him, is satisfied with the easier and safer life of a perennial shirker. He is torn to his very soul by the realization; if it has not been clear to him every single minute, it is when some accidental circumstance sweeps away the fog of forgetfulness and the task unfulfilled stands before him in painful clarity.

The two soliloquies and the events which occasion them may be cited as the most obvious refutation to the theory that external circumstances prevent Hamlet from acting. I cite them first here because they *are* fairly obvious and because they follow logically from that peculiar change of heart noted in the ghost scene. But there is a sequence of events between them which is not quite so obvious, but which, when examined closely, indicates a pattern of behavior on the part of Hamlet which conforms exactly to what he has himself already confessed. The soliloquies constitute an awareness, or consciousness, in Hamlet's own mind that he has shirked a disagreeable duty. But the fact that he is conscious of it, while it is undeniable as evidence, may involve a difficulty: is Hamlet *too willing* to accuse himself? Everything I have said relies entirely on what Hamlet says of himself and to himself. Is he completely trustworthy? Might not excessive humility, or a refusal to accept any excuse for failing to accomplish his end, result in exaggerated self-accusation? Hamlet does, after all, speak humbly of himself on a number of occasions in no way connected with the main theme, and it is possible to make out a case for his general tendency to belittle himself, all of which would militate against a blanket acceptance of the two soliloquies already discussed. Possibly. But the answer to this is that Shakespeare has skillfully exhibited his hero in a series of scenes in which his behavior subconsciously reveals what it consciously reveals elsewhere.

Hamlet is recalled to the path of duty (Act II, Sc. ii) when he realizes that an emotion he ought to feel in reality, is not even as strong as that which he has just witnessed a player acting out. The scene closes with his resolving to put on the play and see if the King behaves guiltily when confronted with a re-enactment of the crime. There is no question of his determination here, following as it does the scathing self-denunciation for having done nothing so far. However, in the very next scene Hamlet appears again, wandering by himself and delivering as soon as he comes on stage the most famous of all Shakespearian soliloquies. I realize that it is very

37

well known to all readers, but I would like to reproduce it here in its entirety, begging the reader to keep in mind as he reads it that the last time we saw the Prince he was berating himself for indifference toward his murdered father and resolved then and there to set about catching his murderer.

> To be, or not to be — that is the question.
> Whether 'tis nobler in the mind to suffer
> The slings and arrows of outrageous fortune,
> Or to take arms against a sea of troubles
> And by opposing end them. To die, to sleep —
> No more, and by a sleep to say we end
> The heartache and the thousand natural shocks
> That flesh is heir to. 'Tis a consummation
> Devoutly to be wished. To die, to sleep,
> To sleep — perchance to dream. Aye, there's the rub,
> For in that sleep of death what dreams may come
> When we have shuffled off this mortal coil
> Must give us pause. There's the respect
> That makes calamity of so long life.
> For who would bear the whips and scorns of time,
> The oppressor's wrong, the proud man's contumely,
> The pangs of despised love, the law's delay,
> The insolence of office and the spurns
> That patient merit of the unworthy takes,
> When he himself might his quietus make
> With a bare bodkin? Who would fardels bear,
> To grunt and sweat under a weary life,
> But that the dread of something after death,
> The undiscovered country from whose bourn
> No traveler returns, puzzles the will,
> And makes us rather bear those ills we have
> Than fly to others that we know not of?
> Thus conscience does make cowards of us all,
> And thus the native hue of resolution
> Is sicklied o'er with the pale cast of thought,
> And enterprises of great pitch and moment
> With this regard their currents turn awry
> And lose the name of action.

I have read opinions which say that this is good poetry but that it has no place in the play, since a prince would hardly have had an experience with the evils and hardships of everyday life. The same defense can be made of this as of the first soliloquy, in that Hamlet is merely generalizing beyond his own experience. The point is, why is he generalizing? What state of mind gives rise to this *taedium vitae* philosophy at this precise point of the play? The means of determining the King's guilt have been put into the Prince's hands and the hour is steadily approaching. Ought not he to be looking forward to it impatiently, dwelling on that one thing above all other things? Yet here he is, weary of it all and acutely conscious of the things that make life painful rather than happy, expressing again that almost-desire to end it and escape but for "that something after death" which prevents such a course.

We need not labor the point of what is so palpable. Those who say Hamlet was prevented from acting in the first place because of the problem of proving the King's guilt, overlook this clear change of heart directly after he has found a way to prove it. The whole tenor of this soliloquy is a cry from the depths of a soul suffering under life's afflictions—evil enough when Hamlet could remain passive under their blows (as in the first soliloquy) but doubly so when he must act in spite of them. These two soliloquies are almost parallel in what they express: life is not worth living, but the laws of God (in the first case) and the fear of what may come after death (in the second) force him to accept life notwithstanding. As Hamlet recoiled from sadness and disappointment at the opening, he recoils from the disagreeable duty he must undertake now. But there is a tiredness or soul-weariness about this soliloquy which is different from Hamlet's reactions at the beginning of the play. When the wounds spoken of in the first soliloquy were still fresh, and when the awful mission of vengeance was first put upon him, the recoil in each instance was sharply spoken. Compare the anguish of that first soliloquy, or of "Oh, cursed spite that ever I was born to set it right!" with the spiritual monotony of "To be or not to be" now that neither suffering nor painful duty is new but each equally difficult to bear. Weariness and the desire to escape characterize it all the way through. We must understand this state of mind in which we find the Prince at this particular time if we are to make any sense at all of the next thing that takes place. He suddenly breaks off his meditations as he notices the presence of Ophelia for the first time, and a rather surprising sequence follows.

Hamlet's treatment of Ophelia at this point has been called brutal, and indeed it is, though not to be wondered at if we correctly read the tortured state of mind he is in. The famous soliloquy was *not* mere philosophical woolgathering. With events both previous and to come very much on Hamlet's mind he did not stop all of a sudden to analyze very dispassionately the problems of mankind. Our frequent reading and hearing this soliloquy out of context has served only to increase its apparent extraneousness, or, if we read it in context, we settle back and go over a familiar passage as a kind of pleasurable experience all by itself. Keeping in mind this new change of heart which turns Hamlet's sense of duty at this point to an enervating escapism, the audience may see in his sentiments the explanation for his treatment of Ophelia. Before taking that up, however, I would like to pause long enough to differ with J. Dover Wilson's opinion that the sight of Ophelia reminds Hamlet of nothing except "the pangs of disprized love," and that he is cold and ironical with her from the start.[4] It is true that Ophelia has, in obedience to her father's commands, rejected Hamlet's attentions over a period of time. Thus it would seem quite reasonable that he, a cast-off lover, would not greet her with any warmth or tenderness at a time and place like this. Reasonable indeed, particularly with the added possibility that Hamlet divines the meeting as pre-arranged by those who are eavesdropping not far off. But, like many other parts of the play, the very plausibility of interpreting a sequence with only limited relation to the entire story can mislead us. Hamlet is so eloquent in his condemnation of Ophelia, his mother, and all women, that he tends to obscure for us the very reason why he sought Ophelia's love in the first place. As she appeared then, she appears now. She is not devoid of the sanctuarized charm which drew him to her when the world became an immoral prison to him, however she may have let him down afterward. The question is the probability of Hamlet's being coldly and bitterly analytical at the sight of her, as opposed to his being lost in such a flood of unhappy feeling that he seeks relief from that only, without concrete thoughts of past and future. The soliloquy he has just uttered is clearly in that vein. He says not a word of what has happened or what is going to happen. His thoughts are abstractions of what most affects him, and when he turns and sees Ophelia his first words indicate a definite change of mood, not a particularizing of what he has been thinking:

> Soft you now!
> The fair Ophelia! Nymph, in thy orisons
> Be all my sins remembered.

The "fair Ophelia" and the "nymph" and the reference to her prayers and his sins are neither cold nor cynical, but a spontaneous utterance from a soul in affliction. How we ruin the effect of this and of what follows if we read it in any other way! Hamlet turns to her as to a sweet angel come upon him in his deepest vexation, and asks that she remember him in her prayers.

It is by no means likely that Ophelia is actually praying or reading a prayer book when Hamlet sees her. This arrangement designed to fit the reference to her "orisons" detracts from the power of what Hamlet expresses, an active thing with him which should not be plucked from him with the aid of stage props. Whatever Ophelia may have lacked in the recent past, at this moment she is again that beautiful contrast with the rest of his world, one whom he has touching need of and before whom he would well prove a humble suppliant.

OPH. Good my lord,
How does your Honor for this many a day?
HAML. I humbly thank you—well, well, well.
OPH. My lord, I have remembrances of yours
That I have longed long to redeliver.
I pray you now receive them.

It is only after this action by Ophelia that Hamlet becomes abusive, a fact that would be pointless if she had reminded him of nothing except "the pangs of disprized love" from the moment he saw her. Certainly it is this return of his presents that prompts his abuse, rather than his first glimpse of her, and this sudden change in Hamlet's demeanor must presuppose an entirely different state of mind just prior to it. If he had expected something like this before it happened, his reaction to it would not be so explosive. I won't say it is a stark tragedy, since it is not the first rebuff from the maid he loves, but we can imagine him in a moment of troubled forgetfulness turning to her again and, instead of deriving whatever comfort he may have hoped for, receives the full impact of her final and definite refusal of his love. She has come to return the tokens of that love. Hamlet knows not what to say, but says nonetheless, "No, not I. I never gave you aught." It is a senseless reply, an incoherent reply that would, if it could, deny all that could bring about this unhappy result. He is in a state of mind to deny, to wish away this final straw. But Ophelia is irritatingly factual in her innocent surprise at his reply.

OPH. My honored lord, you know right well you did,
And with them words of so sweet breath composed
As made the things more rich. Their perfume lost,
Take these again, for to the noble mind
Rich gifts wax poor when givers prove unkind.
There, my lord.
HAML. Ha, ha! Are you honest?
OPH. My lord?
HAML. Are you fair?
OPH. What means your lordship?

> HAML. That if you be honest and fair, your honesty
> should admit no discourse to your beauty.

In a less troubled state of mind Hamlet might have behaved differently to Ophelia. Certainly there are numerous examples in Shakespeare of courtly lovers whose love
is rejected and who do not react by raging at the objects
of their affection. And it seems all the stranger in
Hamlet: he of the "noble mind," the "observed of all
observers." He brutally asks her if she is honest, i.e.,
chaste, and he rants at her in a way that goes beyond
all bounds of seemliness. Yet the very grossness of Hamlet's aspersions cannot be viewed as senseless eruptions
from a youth we would have presumed to be courtly and
chivalrous. What he says does not spring only from
the return of his presents, but from a combination of
that and something else which sorely vexes his mind. It
is true that Ophelia is shocked beyond comprehension;
indeed, why should she comprehend what she does not
suspect? She judges him simply as a lover unalloyed
with any other role. But the King, who has overheard,
is a little more divining:

> There's something in his soul
> O'er which his melancholy sits on brood,
> And I do doubt the hatch and the disclose
> Will be some danger. . . .
> Haply the seas and countries different
> With variable objects shall expel
> *This something-settled matter in his heart*
> *Whereon his brains still beating puts him thus*
> *From fashion of himself.*

My purpose in bringing all this in is to demonstrate the
attitude of Hamlet toward a duty which he does not
want to perform, but which honor, circumstances, and
chance all require that he perform whether he likes it
or not. This duty is not mentioned in the succession of
events we are now looking at, but it is very much on
Hamlet's mind and causes him to become irritable and
tempestuous when other torments are added to it. It is

not a mind that longs to perform the duty it dwells upon, but one filled with grim forebodings as the course of events goes inexorably forward.

Since the soliloquy was a form of letting the audience know a person's thoughts, and was not considered to be actually given aloud (except in those instances in which another person hears what is being said and makes comments on it), it is certainly to be concluded that the King didn't overhear the soliloquy and consequently his view of Hamlet is not as complete as ours. Yet even he could see that something was bothering the Prince which put him "from the fashion of himself." The fact that the King says, "Love! His affections do not that way tend," need not be taken as evidence that Hamlet did not love Ophelia, or that, granting Hamlet did love her, the King is mistaken in saying, "His affections do not that way tend," and consequently just as likely to be mistaken in his surmise that Hamlet is pondering something darkly unsettling. The Prince does not behave in this scene like a man in love, or even like an unrequited lover. The King has had only Polonius' word for it that the Prince is in love with Ophelia, and the context of this scene would hardly bear it out. What Hamlet says is not motivated solely by love unrequited but by something else as well, and this "something else" is the weightier of the two. The King can see that. At least he can see that, taken as a love scene—even an unhappy love scene—it is too incongruous, too inexplicable. There *must* be other reasons. And these other reasons are the root explanation of the admittedly blameable display of temper which seems to lessen Hamlet's stature in our eyes, and in the scenes following they explain as well a number of things which at first glance appear disconnected but when taken together form a perfectly consistent pattern of behavior. In case we miss the point of Shakespeare's psychological exhibition of his melancholy hero in this first instance, the comments of the King should drive it home. True, Claudius may suffer from a guilty conscience and tend to be overly suspicious, but he would have no reason at this point for suspecting Hamlet knows him to be a murderer, or if he did suspect this he would hardly reveal his suspicions, even in the most distant way, to Polonious.

Let us now move to the scene directly after the one we have just been considering. It begins with Hamlet's advice to the players, which I do not think has any special bearing on or is particularly indicative of Hamlet's attitude toward his duty. The advice is good sound stage advice, and it does reveal a certain fastidiousness of taste, a certain sensitivity to the arts. It is well worth studying with reference to our conception of the tender and sensitive Prince, but it contains nothing that relates to the phase of his character that I am now examining. Some may read a kind of significance into this since the play is now closer than ever and Hamlet ought to be more on edge than he was in the previous scene. The answer to this lies partly in the fact that he would not be likely to reveal it to the players, and partly in what he does say when they have gone. When Hamlet finishes his instructions to the players they depart to get themselves ready. Polonius comes in with Rosencrantz and Guilderstern, and in reply to Hamlet's question says that the King and Queen will hear the play and will be in presently. Polonius, Rosencrantz and Guilderstern then depart, leaving Hamlet by himself.

HAML. What ho! Horatio!
            (*Enter* HORATIO.)
HOR.   Here, sweet lord, at your service.
HAML. Horatio, thou art e'en as just a man
            As e'er my conversation coped withal.
HOR.   Oh, my dear lord—
HAML.   Nay, do not think I flatter,
            For what advancement may I hope from thee,
            That no revenue hast but thy good spirits
            To feed and clothe thee? Why should the poor be
                  flattered?
            No, let the candied tongue lick absurd pomp
            And crook the pregnant hinges of the knee

Where thrift may follow fawning. Dost thou hear?
Since my dear soul was mistress of her choice
And could of men distinguish, her election
Hath sealed thee for herself. For thou has been
As one in suffering all that suffers nothing,
A man that fortune's buffets and rewards
Hast ta'en with equal thanks. And blest are those
Whose blood and judgment are so well com-
    mingled
That they are not a pipe for fortune's finger
To sound what stop she please. Give me that man
That is not passion's slave, and I will wear him
In my heart's core—aye, in my heart of heart,
As I do thee.

Hamlet is removed from almost everyone in the play
for one reason or another. Horatio is his one close friend
and confidant, the one principal character between whom
and Hamlet there is never the slightest misunderstanding.
It is a happy bit of dramatic relief from the continual
turmoil and frustrating oppositions Hamlet runs into
everywhere else. He may well be thankful for such a
friend as Horatio, but he seems both consciously and subconsciously grateful because of the type of character
his friend possesses. He sees it and he envies it. Horatio,
ever constant and firm regardless of the buffetings of
nature, is what Hamlet would like to be. How different
must be Horatio's acceptance of life from that revealed
by Hamlet in the To-be-or-not-to-be soliloquy. We, the
spectators, do not know what problems Horatio has had
to face in his lifetime, but in Hamlet's eyes—and Hamlet
would not be completely ignorant in this regard—he is
one who in suffering all suffers nothing. We have seen
two notable instances in which Hamlet was humiliated
in comparing himself with others. The player who performed in a fiction and the band of soldiers ready to risk
their lives for a paltry piece of land, both turn Hamlet's
mind upon himself and the comparison is mortifying.
Now, the unflattering contrast Hamlet is conscious of in
these two instances is just as true with respect to Hora-

tio, and Hamlet appears to be just as much aware of it. But there is a significant difference. Where Hamlet is shamefully humiliated in the other two cases, in this one he is comforted. Where the other two made him see his own deficiencies, this makes him applaud another's virtues.

We can account for this psychological difference only if we remember the different circumstances. In the other two instances Hamlet was comfortably but dishonorably away from the path of duty. I say "comfortably" only in a relative sense, because while I realize he had been "thinking too precisely" the second time, the greatest blow was the realization he was doing nothing. It pricked his conscience. At the present time, however, there is nothing for him to be conscience-stricken about. He is *on* the path of duty, but, as indicated all along, uneasy about it. The two states of mind reveal the Prince as a man never happy when shirking a painful duty, never at ease when undertaking it. Conscience and weakness are continually at war with one another, first one possessing him and then the other. Weakness afflicts him every moment he is engaged in what he should be doing, and finally drives him away from it altogether. But conscience drives him back again. We may look for evidences of one or the other, depending upon whether Hamlet is on his mission or away from it.

Consequently, Hamlet's feeling about Horatio's equanimity and self-command, while it might have been said at any time, is particularly revealing when expressed just before the play is to be put on. There is no doubt that a friend like Horatio is particularly comforting to have at this moment when Hamlet is to undertake the dangerous game of torturing the King's conscience; if Hamlet has always valued Horatio as a friend and as a man he is particularly aware of the other's needful qualities at this awful moment. It is no vulgar fear on the part of Hamlet, no wish to unload disagreeable responsibilities on someone more capable of bearing them. It is the comfort of companionship. It is that strength we all derive from the presence of another person in a moment of danger, even though the danger may be in no way lessened by his being there. Horatio may be of no practical advantage, but his constancy is something that Hamlet nevertheless feels within his own soul. The Prince's praise is not that from a man who admires qualities in another which he has himself; we know that Hamlet does not possess the qualities he is so keenly aware of in Horatio and which he praises at a time when they are very much needed. And this is followed with the information that Hamlet has already taken Horatio into his confidence and will ask his assistance in determining the guilt or innocence of the King:

> There is a play tonight before the King.
> One scene of it comes near the circumstance
> Which I have told thee of my father's death.
> I prithee when thou seest that act afoot,
> Even with the very comment of thy soul
> Observe my uncle. If his occulted guilt
> Do not itself unkennel in one speech
> It is a damned ghost that we have seen
> And my imaginations are as foul
> As Vulcan's stithy. Give him heedful note,
> For I mine eyes will rivet to his face,
> And after we will both our judgments join
> In censure of his seeming.

The scholarly problems relating to the performance of the play, as well as its prominence as a dramatic highlight in the course of avenging justice, have tended to obscure this entire preliminary scene between Hamlet and Horatio. It has its puzzling aspect in that, strictly speaking, much of it is not necessary. Hamlet must speak with his friend and inform him of the purpose of the play and the need for Horatio's corroborative eye on the King. It is not improbable that Hamlet has no chance to explain this to Horatio before now, since the whole strategem occurred to Hamlet only with the arrival of the players the day before and he has doubtless been busy since then coaching them and arranging the play. Moreover, Shakespeare wished to have Hamlet concur with Horatio on stage, both before and after the play, in order that we, the audience, be fully enlightened. It is Hamlet's praise, however, his words of warm admiration which form no integral part of all this, that seem, at a casual reading, to be as extraneous as the To-be-or-not-to-be soliloquy. Neither fits logically into an outline of the progressing action, nor are they to be explained by anything we see taking place. They issue, rather, from Hamlet's own reaction to the march of events, and they, together with his stormy eruption at Ophelia, are dissimilar emotions which confirm the same thing. But because the forthright statement of admiring friendship is more palatable than the other two, it is not therefore less surprising than they are. The fact that both Hamlet and Horatio betray a kind of embarrassment, "Oh, my dear lord—" and Hamlet interrupts himself with "Something too much of this," demonstrates that each man realizes the warm encomium to be, in the discernible circumstances of the moment at least, flowingly gratuitous. It is not that we question Hamlet's characterization of Horatio. It is a thoroughly just analysis. A cruder dramatist than Shakespeare would have had Hamlet exaggerate beyond all truth so as to attract every bit of attention to the state of his mind. This indeed would have pointed up the device, but only at the expense of clouding to some extent the character of Horatio and what draws Hamlet to him. The device should be apparent enough as it is, and once it is seen its purpose cannot be mistaken. That Hamlet speaks in this vein at all, and at this precise moment, establishes another link in the chain of reflexes to his resumed sense of duty. Furthermore, its close connection with the next succeeding link is such as to excite our anticipation of whatever it may prove to be. What will Hamlet be like during the crisis itself, we wonder, as the sound of trumpets halts his conversation with Horatio and ominously announces the approach of the King and Queen and other members of the court. The moment has arrived. The play is about to begin.

Many readers may be puzzled over why Hamlet is in such a merry mood as all the courtly spectators are assembling to hear the play, and even during the performance of the play itself. He is certainly aware of the awful import of what is taking place. And the play, if it may be expected to upset the King in his guilt, must also touch Hamlet in some way as the reenactment of the murder of his father. Yet his behavior appears strange in the extreme. He jokes with Polonius and with Ophelia. He makes humorous remarks about the play. I hardly think the strengthening presence of Horatio can account for it, though I would not disregard it entirely. If Hamlet was so upset at the approach of the fatal moment, why is he so unquestionably lighthearted now that it has arrived? It is true that this lightheartedness disappears somewhat as the play proceeds, but it returns again when the play is over and all the company have left in confusion.

First of all we must remember that we do not see Hamlet afraid to face a situation once it comes upon him, or he upon it. I have spoken continually of Hamlet's weakness, not his lack of courage. Once confronted, he acts. Most of the instances that scholars have cited to prove Hamlet's courage are situations brought upon him rather than brought about by him. It seems that the more he must do and the more remote the doing of it may be, the more difficulty he undergoes in keeping himself to it. Thinking is definitely a roadblock to him and he acts more easily when he does not have too much time to think. Some may object and say he had ample time to think about the ghost before courageously following it and listening to it. I would not absolutely rule out Hamlet's ability to act firmly, even where he does have time to think about it beforehand. The play within the play, for all the turmoil it causes in Hamlet's mind, must be taken as an instance of this. Nevertheless, it would be well to remember that Hamlet hears about the ghost for the first time during the day and goes to meet it that night, not a great deal of time to think about it; and while he suspects that the ghost's appearance bodes some foul play, he has no inkling of what it is going to impose upon him.

It is an admitted fact that worrying over something that must be undergone is often worse than the ordeal itself. It is quite common to wish to face something as soon as possible rather than prolong and worsen the dread of facing it. Many a man has felt a profound sense of relief when the crisis is actually at hand. Sometimes there is good reason for this dread by anticipation, sometimes not. Once it is over, however, at least some part of the total ordeal is lifted and there is a consequent upsurge of spirits. A man of greater constancy and firmness of purpose than Hamlet, someone more like Horatio, would not have felt this lightheartedness on such an occasion. He would not have felt depressed or anticipative in the first place, and there would be no resultant sense of relief when the depression period was at an end. What is not suffered cannot be relieved. Hamlet the moody, the reflective, the tender in one important way, has come through a kind of torment that touches him in a most sensitive place; and since bringing himself to act is more difficult for him than acting itself, this reaction from the one is understandable enough. It may exhibit itself in unexpected ways and at unexpected times, but the condition of mind from whence it emanates, though complex, is perfectly coherent. These changes of behaviour are subtle indications by the great poet of the way Hamlet's mind works, its strengths, its weaknesses, its sensitivities, its tautness under pressure; and its strange, almost gabbling hilarity when it experiences momentary release. And it is pertinent that Shakespeare withholds much that he might say. He who could have his characters speak with such directness and truth, has pictured in this play a man who does not understand himself, a man often not fully cognizant of his own actions till they have already taken place. Is it any wonder that Hamlet does not comment on many of his own alterations of mind (though others do! Remember that. Ophelia speaks of his merry mood half a dozen times in this instance), that he does not say to himself, "Methinks I feel a strange relief come creeping o'er my spirits," or words to that effect? He cannot see—at least not to the point where it can be called *conscious awareness*—his own mind going through its peculiar transformations. It is the psychology of all of us that it is easier for us to see ourselves in retrospect when we have had time to analyze ourselves, than to form simultaneous judgments while our actions, particularly our subconscious depressions and exhilerations, are taking place. Where Hamlet is consciously thinking, he soliloquizes. When he is not, he speaks and acts in a way that is equally revealing. It is significant that Shakespeare has avoided the soliloquy during this sequence of action, even though there is a perfect opportunity for one prior to the play when Polonius, Rosencrantz, and Guildenstern leave him and he is alone on stage.

Now, it might be objected that Hamlet is putting on this merriment purposely to throw the King off the scent; that is to say, he is forcing a jocularity he does not feel in order that the King may be taken unawares. This can hardly be the reason. Claudius has no suspicion of the play before it begins, and once it does begin he is bound to become suspicious regardless of how Hamlet has behaved. In addition, far from concealing his design, Hamlet seems to want to hint it very broadly when he replies to the King's question as to what the play is called:

> *The Mousetrap.* Marry, how? Tropically. This play is the image of a murder done in Vienna. Gonzago is the Duke's name, his wife, Baptista. You shall see anon. 'Tis a knavish

piece of work, but what o' that? Your Majesty, and we that have free souls, it touches us not. Let the galled jade wince, our withers are unwrung.

Some may adopt the very opposite theory, that Hamlet's merriment *is* forced, but for the very opposite reason: to confront the King more openly with some show of carefree conscience as opposed to the guilty one the latter must feel within himself; or else a kind of bravado that sings as it bears down on its anxious foe, a more formidable thing in its way than dead seriousness would be. To all such theories that support Hamlet's behaviour here as forced, and for whatever reason, I can only give my reasons for rejecting them. Hamlet gives us no clue that he will put a forced disposition on, as it is his custom to do when adopting some mode of behaviour. It is true that just before the entry of all the others he says to Horatio, "I must be idle," which in some texts is explained as "I must seem crazy." Like many other words, "idle" had a variety of meanings in Elizabethan times. While there are many instances in which it means "foolish," or "unintelligible," I can recall no instance of it having so strong a meaning as "crazy" or "insane." The only reason we would have for supposing it to mean "crazy" here would come from the belief that Hamlet means to put his antic disposition on once again, i.e., affect insanity. While it would seem that he ought to do this now, since everyone he might wish to impress with his insanity is present, he *does not act crazy* before or during the play. Let us read the colloquy just prior to the play from the time the King and Queen enter with all the others:

KING.   How fares our cousin Hamlet?
HAML.   Excellent, i' faith, of the chameleon's dish.
        I eat the air, promise-crammed. You cannot
        feed capons so.
KING.   I have nothing with this answer, Hamlet.
        These words are not mine.
HAML.   No, nor mine now. (*To* POLONIUS) My lord,

	you played once i 'the university, you say?
POL.	That did I, my lord, and was accounted a good actor.
HAML.	What did you enact?
POL.	I did enact Julius Caesar. I was killed i' the Capitol. Brutus killed me.
HAML.	It was a brute part of him to kill so capital a calf there. Be the players ready?
ROS.	Aye, my lord, they stay upon your patience.
QUEEN.	Come hither, my dear Hamlet, sit by me.
HAML.	No, good Mother, here's metal more attractive.
POL.	(*To the* KING) Oh ho! Do you mark that?
HAML.	Lady, shall I lie in your lap?
	(*Lying down at* OPHELIA'S *feet*)
OPH.	No, my lord.
HAML.	I mean, my head upon your lap?
OPH.	Aye, my lord.
HAML.	Do you think I meant country matters?
OPH.	I think nothing, my lord.
HAML.	That's a fair thought to lie between maids' legs.
OPH.	What is, my lord?
HAML.	Nothing.
OPH.	You are merry, my lord.
HAML.	Who, I?
OPH.	Aye, my lord.
HAML.	Oh God, your only jig-maker. What should a man do but be merry? For look you how cheerfully my mother looks, and my father died within's two hours.
OPH.	Nay, 'tis twice two months, my lord.
HAML.	So long? Nay, then, let the Devil wear black, for I'll have a suit of sables. Oh heavens! Die two months ago, and not forgotten yet? Then there's hope a great man's memory may outlive his life half a year. But, by 'r Lady, he must build churches then, or else shall he suffer not thinking on, with the hobbyhorse, whose epitath is "For, oh, for oh, the hobbyhorse is forgot."

There is no indication of pretended insanity here, with the exception of Hamlet's one remark to Ophelia about his father being dead within two hours, and that can easily be interpreted as a bit of nonsense with no particular importance attached. There being no further remarks to corroborate this one as additional instances of assumed insanity, it is difficult to see how a case can be made for it. His remark, "I eat the air, promise-crammed. You cannot feed capons so," which the King either does not understand or pretends not to understand, actually does make sense; and it is easy to fathom why the King affects to be able to make nothing of it. Hamlet jokes with Polonius. He is flippant with his mother. He is both merry and bawdy with Ophelia. After the play begins his remarks are addressed mainly to Ophelia, still in the same merry and bawdy vein. There is a very brief colloquy with the King and Queen which certainly reveals no attempt to feign insanity:

> HAML. Madam, how like you this play?
> QUEEN. The lady doth protest too much, methinks.
> HAML. Oh, but she'll keep her word.
> KING. Have you heard the argument? Is there no
> offense in 't?
> HAML. No, no, they do but jest, poison in jest—
> no offense i' the world.

From the time of the arrival of everyone until the time they depart in confusion, never once does Hamlet's conversation become incoherent, or suggest assumed insanity—an assumed insanity undeniably present on at least one previous occasion. And Ophelia's comments, "You are merry, my lord," "You are naught, you are naught," "You are as good as a chorus, my lord," "You are keen, my lord, you are keen," "Still better, and worse," do not suggest she thinks him deranged here. Nor is she acting the role of one who tactfully passes over the insane conversation of another with pleasantries, since she takes seriously his one senseless remark and corrects him:

> HAML.   For look you how
> cheerfully my mother looks, and my
> father died within 's two hours.

OPH.   Nay, 'tis twice two months, my lord.

None of the others give the slightest indication that they see anything insane about the Prince's talk. Polonius calls the attention of the King to Hamlet's remark about Ophelia, not because the remark itself can in any way be construed as insane, but because Polonius has always believed the Prince's "insanity" to be the result of disappointed love and is ready to read his every reference to Ophelia as meaningful in this connection.

But to return to Hamlet's remark to Horatio prior to the gathering of all to witness the play, he does say, "I must be idle." Granted it may not mean crazy; it must mean something, and he says, "I *must* be," meaning it is necessary for him to act in some way or other, which would argue against his behavior being purely natural and unaffected. Not necessarily. The very brief remark, taken by itself, is subject to various interpretations, and the logical one would be that which fits all angles of the situation in which it occurs. If Hamlet said, "I must *seem*," instead of "I must *be*," there would be more grounds for thinking his behaviour mere show. "I must be idle" need connote no more than it would in any instance where a person expects a company of people very shortly and adopts a fitting demeanor in which to receive them, a demeanor which would still allow a variety of moods. Hamlet says, "They are coming to the play. I must be idle. Get you a place." This undoubtedly refers to the way he will comport himself as the others are entering the room to witness a play to which the Prince has invited them. He must adopt a company manner for the occasion, not only because he is in a sense the host to all present, but in order not to awaken the King's suspicions at the outset and so put him on his guard. But as I said before, the King's suspicions are bound to become aroused during the course of the play and Hamlet's merriment continues long after the King would be expected to get the first inkling of this re-enactment of his crime, and even after the King gives the first positive indication of his suspicions:

> KING.   Have you heard the argument? *Is there no offense in 't?*

This company manner, or idle manner, which Hamlet adopts should not lead us to dismiss the mood he is obviously in as being in no sense adopted at all. As I say, even an adopted demeanor may allow for a variety of moods. Any person on some public occasions may reveal a particular mood without ceasing to behave in a manner proper to that occasion.

But I scarcely believe I have yet proved that Hamlet's behavior in this scene is in the main natural and spontaneous. Accept the term "idle," then, in any sense of the word and say that Hamlet affects his behavior for some purpose. What possible purpose could he have for continuing in the same vein after all the others have gone and he is alone with his friend Horatio? We would certainly expect him to drop the merry mood then, if it were merely put on. Whatever reason can be adduced for its adoption in the first place, would no longer stand; and it seems strange indeed that Hamlet who now has proof of the King's guilt is not in a more deadly serious, a grimmer state of mind. He jokes. He gives sportive imitations of an actor for Horatio's amusement. All this before mentioning a word about the King's guilt and the ghost having been justified—which, incidentally, is little more than mentioned and mentioned very jovially, after which Hamlet gaily calls for music. Rosencrantz and Guildenstern come to tell him the King is marvelous distempered, and also to summon him to his mother. He cannot be serious with them. It is as if he cannot control himself at all. Let us read this much of the scene commencing immediately after the King has interrupted the play and everyone has left except Hamlet and Horatio:

> HAML.   "Why, let the stricken deer go weep,

The hart ungalled play,
For some must watch while some must sleep.
　　Thus runs the world away."
Would not this, sir, and a forest of feathers—
if the rest of my fortunes turn Turk with
me—with two Provincial roses on my razed
shoes, get me a fellowship in a cry of
players, sir?

HOR.　　　Half a share.

HAML.　　A whole one, I.
"For thou dost know, O Damon dear,
　　This realm dismantled was
Of Jove, himself, and now reigns here
　　A very, very—pajock."

HOR.　　　You might have rhymed.

HAML.　　O good Horatio, I'll take the ghost's word
for a thousand pound. Didst perceive?

HOR.　　　Very well, my lord.

HAML.　　Upon the talk of the poisoning?

HOR.　　　I did very well note him.

HAML.　　Ah, ha! Come, some music! Come, the
recorders!
"For if the King like not the comedy,
why then, belike, he likes it not, perdy."
Come, some music!

　　　　(*Re-enter* ROSENCRANTZ *and* GUILDENSTERN.)

GUIL.　　Good my lord, vouchsafe me a word with you.

HAML.　　Sir, a whole history.

GUIL.　　The King, sir—

HAML.　　Aye, sir, what of him?

GUIL.　　Is in his retirement marvelous distempered.

HAML.　　With drink, sir?

GUIL.　　No, my lord, rather with choler.

HAML.　　Your wisdom should show itself more richer
to signify this to the doctor, for for me to
put him to his purgation would perhaps
plunge him into far more choler.

GUIL.　　Good my lord, put your discourse into some
frame, and start not so wildly from my
affair.

HAML.　　I am tame, sir. Pronounce.

GUIL.　　The Queen your mother, in most great
affliction of spirit, hath sent me to you.

HAML.　　You are welcome.

GUIL.　　Nay, good my lord, this courtesy is not of

<blockquote>

the right breed. If it shall please you
to make me a wholesome answer, I will do
your mother's commandment. If not, your
pardon and my return shall be the end of my
business.

HAML.   Sir, I cannot.

GUIL.   What, my lord?

HAML.   Make you a wholesome answer, my wit's
diseased. But, sir, such answer as I can
make you shall command, or rather, as you
say, my mother. Therefore no more, but
to the matter. My mother, you say—

ROS.   Then thus she says. Your behavior hath
struck her into amazement and admiration.

HAML.   Oh, wonderful son that can so astonish a
mother! But is there no sequel at the
heels of this mother's admiration? Impart.

ROS.   She desires to speak with you in her closet
ere you go to bed.

HAML.   We shall obey, were she ten times our
mother. Have you any further trade with us?

</blockquote>

Now, all this seems, at a casual reading, to be unaccountable deportment in a man who has just secured proof against the murderer of his father. Unless we see into the character of the man and read his behavior in the light of fine psychological reactions to events as they happen, it reads like just so many disconnected moods. We are left with that catch-all, Hamlet's insanity (or feigned insanity), which conveniently gathers all his strange actions under one heading and leaves them there.

Those who will object to my explanation of Hamlet's lightheartedness before and during the play, may do so again on the grounds that, when the play is over, Hamlet has reason to be glad which he did not have previously: the success of his exploit. Yet it is exactly this that looks so odd. His joy is not so much gratification that his plan succeeded—since he scarcely mentions it—but an almost uncontrollable frolic, a boyish exuberance, a kind of tail-wagging. It is not like Hamlet to be merry. Why is he so at this particular time? Compare his behavior here with that of anyone of a number of Shakespearian characters who find themselves in somewhat similar circumstances. How different is the manner of Prince Henry when he realizes the die is cast and he must redeem his honor upon the head of young Henry Percy. Compare his speech to his father in Act III, Sc. ii, of the First Part of *Henry IV*, with the foolery of Hamlet when the latter undoubtedly has an equal realization (if he thinks seriously upon it) that the course is set and righteous vengeance must be executed. Or compare the behavior of Benedick when set on by Beatrice to avenge the wrong done to Hero, a duty which Benedick certainly shrank from at the outset. Compare the deadly determination of Macduff from the time he hears of the slaughter of his wife and children, right through the moment when he at last faces Macbeth on the battlefield. These others are brought to a point where a terrible reckoning must be gone through with. Prince Henry and Benedick, though usually inclined to merriment, become deadly serious when honor is at stake, and though the former shows a kind of exultation when contemplating what he will do, he does not become prankish or exuberant. Macduff, always serious, remains so to the critical moment.

If Hamlet betrays anxiety and shrinking from dread duty where these others show forceful determination, and if he betrays a similarly contrasting merriment where they continue to be serious, the explanation becomes almost obvious. Hamlet's ebullience of spirits is because one ordeal, one step of duty is over with, and not because another is closer. The release from the thing itself is doubly as pleasant as the release from the anticipation of it; and Hamlet's buoyancy is far more pronounced after the play than it was just prior to and during it. There is scarcely a hint that it is due to the fact that his plan has succeeded and his duty is now plainly cut out for him. Furthermore, while Hamlet does become more serious toward the end of this scene, it is because he resents the attempts of Rosencrantz, Guildenstern, and Polonius to draw his secret out of him. He does not trust any of them, knowing full well they will report to the King anything they are able to learn. Rosencrantz and Guildenstern insist it is their love for the Prince that bids them speak, and that they are grieved that he treats them with such clowning evasions. Whether they are telling the truth or not, Hamlet does not believe them. He remembers that some time ago they had been sent for by the King in order to be spies and informers, and he can hardly take seriously their assertion now that it is their love for him (rather than the King's anxiety) that prompts their conern. Hamlet takes up a musical instrument and asks Guildenstern to play upon it.

GUIL. My lord, I cannot.
HAML. I pray you.
GUIL. Believe me, I cannot.
HAML. I do beseech you.
GUIL. I know no touch of it, my lord.
HAML. It is as easy as lying. Govern these
ventages with your fingers and thumb,
give it breath with your mouth, and it
will discourse most eloquent music.
Look you, these are the stops.
GUIL. But these cannot I command to any utterance of harmony, I have not the skill.
HAML. Why, look you now, how unworthy a thing
you make of me! You would play upon me,
you would seem to know my stops, you
would pluck out the heart of my mystery,
you would sound me from my lowest note
to the top of my compass—and there is
much music, excellent voice, in this
little organ—yet cannot you make it
speak. 'Sblood, do you think I am
easier to be played on than a pipe?
Call me what instrument you will, though
you can fret me, you cannot play upon me.

Polonius enters. Hamlet knows perfectly well the old man has no more concern for him than the other two

had, and he says a number of contradictory things just
to see if Polonius will agree with them:

POL.   My lord, the Queen would speak with you,
        and presently.
HAML.   Do you see yonder cloud that's almost
        in shape of a camel?
POL.   By the mass, and 'tis like a camel indeed.
HAML.   Methinks it is like a weasel.
POL.   It is backed like a weasel.
HAML.   Or like a whale?
POL.   Very like a whale.
HAML.   Then I will come to my mother by and
        by. They fool me to the top of my
        bent. I will come by and by.

No doubt their coming from the King associates Hamlet's mind once more with what he must do. But these lines clearly indicate that that association is *brought to* Hamlet and is not the result of his thinking of it himself. This, together with personal resentment at being played upon—"They fool me to the top of my bent"—makes him serious once more. He bids everyone leave him and the scene closes with the short soliloquy:

'Tis now the very witching time of night,
When churchyards yawn and Hell itself breathes out
Contagion to this world. Now could I drink hot blood,
And do such bitter business as the day
Would quake to look on. Soft! Now to my mother.
O heart, lose not thy nature, let not ever
The soul of Nero enter this firm bosom.
Let me be cruel, not unnatural.
I will speak daggers to her, but use none.
My tongue and soul in this be hypocrites,
How in my words soever she be shent,
To give them seals never, my soul, consent!

There is no question about the deadly seriousness of this, particularly in connection with what follows. Hamlet is now alone at dead of night, face to face with the awful imminence of what he must do. One hates to be analytical at this point. The powerfully poetic words are the very essence of the night where vengeance unchained stalks up dark stairs, sword in hand, eyes raised toward him above who is marked for death. Hamlet is almost at one with this stark atmosphere he breathes. The deed he must do appears to him, not in the garb of its justice, not in the light of honor vindicated, not in any of the ways it might appear in other circumstances, or to other people, but as "such bitter business as the day would quake to look on."

But does this "bitter business" apply to Claudius or to Gertrude? Is Hamlet, from the very beginning of this soliloquy, speaking of the visit he must make to his mother in response to her message, and is it she he is thinking of when he says he could drink hot blood? I hardly think so. I am quite certain that the horror thoughts expressed in the first two sentences are concerned with the slaying of the King. When, a few lines later, he cautions himself not to harm his mother, "Let me be cruel, not unnatural," he does not recoil from or banish the opening thoughts, which he would certainly do if he had meant them for her. "Let not ever the soul of Nero enter this firm bosom," he says. But if drinking hot blood meant wounding or slaying his mother, the soul of Nero *had* indeed entered into him, however, momentarily, and we would expect some penitence or self-correction for having had the thought at all. The whole speech is illogical if Hamlet were thinking of no one but his mother all the way through. If the opening part applies to the King and the rest of it to the Queen, the entire speech follows quite logically. After speaking of the vengeance he could do now upon Claudius, the Prince then says, "Soft! Now to my mother." "Soft," "softly," "soft you now," are Elizabethan expressions commonly used when a character interrupts a train of thought and turns his mind to something else. And having mentioned his mother now for the first time in the soliloquy, he purges himself of bloody thoughts in planning how to act toward her; *without,* however, a syllable of regret over having had these bloody thoughts in the first place. To whom could they apply but the King?

Here Hamlet does not exult. He does not feel any sense of gratification which we have looked for in vain elsewhere. He seems almost to have become something demoniacal in his conntemplation now of proof secured, the hour at hand, and sword in readiness. He goes out. He is on his way to his mother, since she has sent for him, but on the way there he turns and steals softly into the King's chamber and finds him at prayer. Right here and at this very moment he may do it. Opportunity, if it were ever lacking in the past, has come.

> Now might I do it pat, now he is praying,
> And now I'll do 't.

Yet, on the very brink of doing the act Hamlet hesitates. He will not do it now, and after rendering reasons to himself he withdraws from the King's chamber.

The reason invariably accepted for Hamlet's refusal to kill the King is the one given by Hamlet himself; that is, to kill the King while he is praying—and presumably repenting of his sins—would be to send his soul to heaven. "Oh, this is hire and salary, not revenge!" reasons Hamlet.

> A villain kills my father, and for that
> I, his sole son, do this same villain send
> To Heaven.

Besides, the King did not give Hamlet's father a chance to repent his sins before killing him.

> He took my father grossly, full of bread,
> With all his crimes broad blown, as flush as May,
> And how his audit stands who knows save Heaven?
> But in our circumstance and course of thought,
> 'Tis heavy with him.

And so Hamlet decides he will wait and kill Claudius when the King has sin on his soul.

> When he is drunk asleep, or in his rage,
> Or in the incestuous pleasure of his bed—

>   At gaming, swearing, or about some act
>   That has no relish of salvation in 't—

These sound like convincing reasons, so convincing that many have taken them quite seriously. Are they adequate, however? Is Hamlet, suddenly confronted with the opportunity of dispatching the King, unable to go through with it, the one time in the play he is unable to meet a situation sprung quickly upon him? Is the opportunity to commit the act the more frightening by it very suddenness, a suddenness intensified by the prior remoteness with which Hamlet has long regarded it, and is Hamlet seeking pretexts for postponing the inevitable? If we seek for reasons beyond mere conjecture, let us remember that the ghost appears to Hamlet in the very next scene, no more than a few minutes—and more probably a matter of seconds—later, and tells him

>   Do not forget. This visitation
>   Is but to whet *thy almost blunted purpose.*

Thy almost blunted purpose! If the ghost, as the events of the play prove, is supernatural and possesses more than worldly knowledge, he must be speaking the truth. And how could Hamlet's purpose be almost blunted if, after securing adequate proof the King is a murderer, his only chance to kill him is thwarted by *very good reasons?* It is true that his purpose was almost blunted in the past, but not now, not when he has progressed nicely right up to bringing himself to put his sword into Claudius's body only to be stopped by circumstances beyond his control. *Provided* these circumstances *do* actually prevent him. If they do, then the ghost's admonition is pointless and his words untrue at this time. A ghostly visit prior to this or later than this would be much more to the point. Moreover, Hamlet guesses the reason for the ghost's visit before the ghost even speaks.

>   Do you not come your tardy son to chide
>   That, lapsed in time and passion, lets go by

The important acting of your dread command?
Oh, say!

We may wonder as to just how conscious Hamlet could have been of the falsity of his reasons for not killing the King at the time he was debating them with himself. He could not have been entirely convinced they were good reasons, because when he is confronted with the ghost he immediately guesses what the message is going to be. On the other hand I do not believe he was deliberately and openly lying to himself when he decided not to kill his uncle. Hamlet's state of mind was that of a person who almost convinces himself, though not entirely; and the unexpected reappearance of his ghostly taskmaster made him sharply aware of what he almost succeeded in stifling within himself by a piece of sophistry. Many have believed Hamlet incapable of entertaining so horible a plan as to send the King's soul to hell, and I am inclined to agree with them. If some other reason for refusing to kill the King had occurred to Hamlet, a reason more in keeping with his character, I might be tempted to think he believed it himself. It is true that Hamlet has Rosencrantz and Guildenstern put to death without "shriving time allowed," but this was a practical matter of not giving them a chance to talk, which— since he could not have foreseen his timely escape by the pirate ship—would have meant his life rather than theirs.

Furthermore, Hamlet's mission must be seen as an act of justice and not a mere satisfaction of personal vengeance. His command to avenge his father's death at most meant to kill the King; nothing was specified about doing it while the King was in a state of mortal sin. If he were to kill Claudius "when he was drunk asleep, or in his rage, or in the incestuous pleasure of his bed—at gaming, swearing, or about some act that has no relish of salvation in 't," it would be for any or all of these sins that the King would undergo future punishment, and not the one revealed to Hamlet at the beginning of the play. This goes beyond Hamlet's specific commission, far beyond it, and the result is that he lets slip a perfect opportunity in order to achieve what is unwarranted. It is true that the King sent the elder Hamlet to his death with unrepented sins on his soul and it might seem like poetic justice to do the same to Claudius. But if the elder Hamlet is "confined to fast in fires till the foul crimes done in my days of nature are burnt and purged away," he is in Purgatory, and, though suffering, is saved.

There has been much dispute about whether Hamlet is himself Protestant or Catholic, a question that bears materially on whether he would believe that there is such a place as Purgatory. Facts which may be adduced to support one view or the other, however, fade into insignificance beside the indisputable revelation that the ghost is in such a place. If we argue that Shakespeare shaped the play to the Protestant views of his Elizabethan audience, that audience could hardly have derived much satisfaction from any supposed views of Hamlet that Purgatory does not exist, when the play itself clearly shows that it does. Hamlet never debates the question, nor does he betray any surprise when the ghost of his father describes the purging torments that are to last only for a time. Since the fate of his father is allegedly the determining factor in Hamlet's postponement of the act of vengeance, the destination of Claudius after death would logically entail three possibilities, not two. That Hamlet does not say anything of this third possibility only argues a deficiency or insincerity of reasoning when he puts up his sword and backs out of the King's chamber, for the reality of Purgatory would have suggested certain things not in keeping with the decision Hamlet formulates. It was not the teaching of those who accepted Purgatory, nor could Hamlet have presumed that it was, that a man would go straight to heaven if killed while in the act of repentence. Sincere repentence brings about forgiveness of sin but does not relieve the temporal punishment due to sin. That must be worked out on earth or cleansed in Purgatory, or both. Hamlet does not specifically say *straight* to heaven, but he does say, "And now I'll do 't. And so he goes to Heaven." He makes no mention of how long it might be before Claudius would arrive there, and it is at least conjecturable that Hamlet meant he would go immediately to heaven. Admit the tenets of the older faith and we not only destroy any such conclusion, but we establish a tentative basis for the fact that Hamlet would have achieved an even justice in sending the King to the same place the elder Hamlet had been sent.

Furthermore, if the eternal punishment for the crime of murder be remitted in heaven by virtue of true sorrow, Hamlet has no warrant for attempting to reinstate it on the basis of additional crimes the King might be expected to commit. Hamlet has no way of knowing how sincere the King's repentence is, naturally, but even if he mistakingly believes it to be sincere this would be understandable error, not a blunting of purpose. The very words of the ghost suggest what Hamlet often imputes to himself: not frustrated desire, but an absence or blunting of desire. And his line of reasoning is simply to excuse the fact. It is a decision seized upon with haste, when we think of other considerations that might have occurred to him.

On top of all this there is the well-known fact that Hamlet kills Polonius believing him to be the King. It is worth while thinking this over. There can be no doubt Hamlet thinks he is killing Claudius when he draws his sword, thrusts it through the arras, and kills someone standing in back of it. Directly after refusing the opportunity of putting Claudius to death, Hamlet goes to his mother's room. Some words pass between him and his mother; she becomes frightened at his threatening manner and cries for help. Polonius, listening behind the arras, evidently believes the Queen to be in danger because he cries for help also, immediately upon hearing which Hamlet whirls and plunges his sword through the arras, saying, "How now! A rat? Dead, for a ducat, dead!" Whether "for a ducat" means "I'll bet a ducat," as explained in some texts, or has some more abstruse meaning, it is clear that Hamlet is pronouncing his victim dead as he stabs him, and that he intends to kill him. It is equally clear that Hamlet believes he is killing the King. His first question is, "Is it the King?" and when he discovers that it is Polonius he says, "Thou wretched, rash, intruding fool, farewell! *I took thee for thy better.*" "Thy better" can only mean the King, the Queen, or Hamlet himself, and since the Queen is right there all the time Hamlet must mean that he took Polonius for Claudius. The King would have had time to get from his room to the Queen's room between the time Hamlet left him praying and the time Polonius cries out from behind the arras.

Now, the question I propose is this: what possible chance would the King have had to commit any of the sins Hamlet has vowed must be on his soul before being sent to face eternal judgment? He has just come from prayer and, so far as Hamlet knows (if we credit his reasons in the first place), is in a state of repentence. It would be extremely unlikely that he would plunge back into serious sin in those few short moments. Even if we stretch a point and say the King could have sinned in the interim, what possible proof could Hamlet have that he had done so? His reasoning would certainly imply that he, Hamlet, must possess good evidence that the King be in a state of sin before he will kill him. Anything less is "hire and salary, not revenge."

Why, then, does Hamlet refuse to kill the King one moment and (as he thinks) kill him the next when, for all he knows, the state of the King's soul is the same both times? The question may answer itself easily enough, but the significance of it needs some pondering. The act of killing is a hasty one. Whatever motive Hamlet has is a motive that comes on the spur of the moment, and his action takes place all in a split second. Whether it is a sudden sense of danger, or a completely thoughtless act, or that Hamlet was capable of doing in a moment of passion what he could not perform in a more calculating frame of mind, may be well nigh impossible to determine. And whatever reason we may decide upon, it can easily be said that since it happens so swiftly we cannot judge too harshly of the deed.

Now, this inconsistency in Hamlet's actions poses another question. If we take the position that Hamlet was wrong in refusing to kill the King in the first place, doesn't it follow that he must have been right in killing him in the second—regardless of the fact that it was a case of mistaken identity? Or if he were wrong the second time, was he not right the first? The ghost does not appear until after Hamlet slays Polonius, and if, as I said, the ghost is right in condemning Hamlet's failure in the face of reasons why he did not kill the King when opportunity presented itself, how can the ghost still be right after Hamlet has killed someone he believed to be the King? The curious paradox of having to prove Hamlet wrong both times must be resolved, partly by appealing to the ghost's "thy almost blunted *purpose*," and partly by keeping in mind the state of Hamlet's determination ever since the soliloquy in which he vowed to catch the conscience of the King. Hamlet could not have been right the second time (if wrong the first) unless he deliberately rejected and repudiated all the reasons he had previously advanced. If he had reversed himself and corrected a set of false reasons, then we could say he had whetted his own blunted purpose. But he does not do this. He does not get the chance. And there is little reason to suppose he would change then and there if he did get the chance. A man is judged according to the motives by which he acts, not by the accidental outcome of his act. If Hamlet killed the King in a sudden rage, or on the spur of the moment, or in what he believed to be danger from the King hiding somewhere, he could not be properly said to have avenged his father's murder. He would be primarily protecting himself, or satisfying his rage, or any one of a number of things which would coincidentally kill the man who murdered his father. And it is by all these things that the ghost judges him when the two meet in the Queen's chamber. Hamlet thrusting his sword through the tapestry and pronouncing the King dead, was *not* obeying that duty enjoined by his ghostly sire: "Remember me!"

It must be injected at this point that, however Hamlet's role of avenger be justified, there is something base in the thought of his stabbing the King in the back. We must remember, nevertheless, that the ghost specified no such action. That Claudius should, as the laws of the time certainly dictated, be put to death for his crime of regicide is a likely and widely accepted conclusion, and it would complicate Hamlet's duty to demand that he confront Claudius with the evil deed and give him time to repent. It would not be impossible in the scene in the King's room. Regardless of how we feel about the precise method Hamlet ought to use, the fact remains that Hamlet himself narrows the action to the simple expedient of using his sword, and then argues his way out of it. Was he right in shying away from what must appear to many as dastardly? If we think it was, we have simply to recall that the means of execution were of Hamlet's own choosing, and the alternative he seems to prefer entails a far more dire method. The very incongruity of the entire situation militates more strongly than ever against the sincerity of his motives in this particular instance.

This insincerity is imperfectly seen, however, unless we take into account the reason for Hamlet's acceptance of the assassin's role in the first place. His long evasion of the act of justice has caused Hamlet to regard that act, subconsciously no doubt, as more and more terrifying. Escape was preferable, but escape was never really possible. The duty left undone "will out," just as surely as the most secret crime. When this duty emerges once more into Hamlet's conscious perception, he views it as a hideous thing that he once put away. Indeed, it is hardly surprising that he envisions according to his own psychological reluctance and frames a monster. The condemnation "Thy almost blunted purpose" is made when Hamlet has been very active, first about catching the conscience of the King and next about castigating his immoral mother. But he does both after a period of comfortable inactivity, and, instead of acting with clear vision and high purpose, he stumbles about in a mass of misdirected drives, empty sophistries, hyperemotional moralizings, and unseemly bursts of gaiety. We can understand these, only if we remember that from the time of the player's speech Hamlet has been controlled by his anxieties. Even in anxieties there is a logic or consistency. Justice may conceive of duty one way. But Hamlet, though laboring to perform the justice demanded of him, allows his mental turmoil to give this justice a horrid and reprehensible shape.

This whole middle section surrounding the play within the play is Shakespeare's most subtle delineation of Hamlet's attitude toward the thing he must perform. Of the three parts of the play which deal principally with this question—the soliloquy in which he plans the play, the play itself, and the final soliloquy—this middle part demands the closest study. Because the soliloquy is such a direct form of imparting character to the audience, we have perhaps become oblivious of the fact that a character who soliloquizes so frequently and at such length as Hamlet does may have less direct and more involved ways of revealing his character. I have read one opinion, for instance, which states that in order to understand Hamlet we need only read the four major soliloquies and study them. This is far from the truth. Not only does it omit the importance of the occasion for each soliloquy and its relationship to the rest of the play, but it ignores the importance of the whole succession of scenes at the very heart of the drama in which we see the Prince in action.

What, then, is to be derived from all this? I must end this chapter on a note of incompleteness, and perhaps on conclusions which will disappoint those who feel a true love of Prince Hamlet. What I have concentrated upon in this chapter is the very worse side of Hamlet's character, and I have tried to see it honestly and through a close scrutiny of everything that has any bearing on it. He *did* shirk his duty. It was a difficult and painful duty to pursue and some excuses may be made for certain minor lapses in his pursuance of it, but his over-all failure to act cannot be condoned. This failure is consistent with his character, but not consistent with right and wrong. Whatever is consistent with character is simply the logic of character portrayal. But what is not consistent with duty cannot be justified. And no one has said so more plainly than Hamlet himself.

III

THINKING
TOO PRECISELY

The question I have so far attempted to decide turns on the so-called "external" and "internal" theories regarding Hamlet's procrastination. That is to say, whether his delay results from circumstances external to himself or within himself must be decided one way or the other, and I believe a careful reading of the play forces us to accept the internal theory. External circumstances present the Prince with difficulties, not impossibilities, and we must conclude that he *fails to act*. He is *not prevented from acting*. But the question remains: why does he fail? Is he a coward? Is he indifferent?

Is he lacking in determination? Is he the tender, sensitive youth Goethe pictures,[5] too delicate to execute so harsh a duty? Before selecting or rejecting any one of these, or even attempting to combine them all into a broader answer, I would like to examine this a little further. It is my belief that a sound and logical reason exists but that it cannot be stated briefly, nor will it be accepted without exhaustive proof. As I have said at the outset, any simple explanation of Hamlet immediately brings to mind many things that will not fit and yet cannot be dispensed with. Unless we make sense of Hamlet as a person we cannot make sense of the play itself.

What we have so far seen of the Prince indicates something of the extremes of thoughtless action on the one hand and actionless thought on the other. If there be any constant pattern in the changes that come over Hamlet, it can be seen with clear relation between one and the other. Whenever he is capable of either action or angry determination to act, he is in a state of high passion where such things come easily; when he seems incapable or unwilling it is after he has had a chance to cool and indulge in thought once more, often unrelated thought. To return for a moment to Hamlet's first interview with the ghost, we see that the revelation of his father's murder brings feelings of rage and determination so well mingled that it is understandable that one can subside when the other does. Listen carefully to Hamlet's words:

> Remember thee!
> Aye, thou poor ghost, while memory holds a seat
> In this distracted globe. Remember thee!
> Yea, from the table of my memory
> I'll wipe away all trivial fond records,
> All saws of books, all forms, all pressures past,
> That youth and observation copied there,
> And thy commandment all alone shall live
> Within the book and volume of my brain,
> Unmixed with baser matter. Yes, by Heaven!

> O most pernicious woman!
> O villain, villain, smiling, damned villain!

It is natural that Hamlet would feel both rage and determination at this point, but one might expect them to come in a kind of sequence, one after the other: uncontrollable anger at what the ghost has revealed to him, followed by a grim determination to do something about it. In this speech they are so interwoven that it is difficult to separate them, unless we select pieces here and pieces there. Hamlet's resolve comes bursting forth in a series of wild interjections, and the reason for this is clearly because his resolve coincides with natural inclination. Any action, any duty is more easily executed when it is in harmony with the personal feelings of the moment. In voicing his rage and his determination at the same time rather than in sequence Hamlet indicates more forcibly the interdependence of the two. It is my guess that had opportunity presented itself right then and there he would have killed the King on the spot. It is only a guess, but I base it not only on the high degree of coincidence of passion and resolve in the Prince's mind at the time, but on the fact that his own words suggest a dim awareness he may feel differently once he has grown calm:

> Hold, hold, my heart,
> And you, my sinews, grow not instant old
> But bear me stiffly up.

No opportunity presents itself, however. His friends arrive and he begins to answer their questions, betraying at first a kind of incoherence and then that tendency to jocularity after a moment of high tension has passed. The ghost has been gone for several minutes, the first glimmerings of morning are becoming more and more pronounced, here are Horatio and Marcellus by his side once more, and Hamlet is lost in thought at the transition from the scarcely credible visit of the ghost of his father and what the ghost has told him, to the stirring of normal life once more. He is no longer enraged. He is confused and wondering, and he is aware of some danger that Horatio and Marcellus may reveal the dread secret if he tells it to them. He starts to say one thing and ends up saying another:

There's ne'er a villain dwelling in all Denmark, he begins, and then finishes in a sudden realization he must check whatever he was going to say: But he's and arrant knave.

Horatio can make nothing of this senseless remark:

> There needs no ghost, my lord, come from the grave
> To tell us this.

This has the effect of recalling Hamlet to himself, though not entirely, as the following lines show:

> HAML. Why, right, you are i' the right.
> And so, without more circumstances at all,
> I hold it fit that we shake hands and part—
> You as your business and desire shall point you,
> For every man hath business and desire,
> Such as it is. And for my own poor part,
> Look you, I'll go pray.
> HOR.   These are but wild and whirling words, by lord.
> HAML. I'm sorry they offend you, heartily,
> Yes, faith, heartily.
> HOR.   There's no offense,
> my lord.

Hamlet's "wild and whirling words" do begin to subside, however, and he becomes his normal self once more. There is a psychological relief as he even jokes with the ghost several times, he cools noticeably, and the scene ends with that totally different attitude in which he curses the fact that he was ever born to right the wrongs of the time he lives in. With the evaporation of his ire his determination has apparently gone with it. This easing off of tension, passion, and determination, is too like Hamlet's reaction after the play to be lightly passed over. If we think him inconsistent his very inconsistency, like his putative madness, has method in it. To know why Hamlet changes from time to time, we must determine what is present or lacking that may be said to assist or retard him in accomplishing certain things.

When Hamlet's conscience is prodded by the player portraying anguish "in a fiction," and he decides once more to be about his duty, there is no feeling of ire (except towards himself), and his determination is a great deal less marked. There is no burning desire to do, but rather a struggle with his own inertia to make himself do. While there is again a kind of agreement between natural inclination and duty, this time the natural inclination comes from a sense of that duty, or moral obligation toward it. This is not the powerful stimulus that was provided before by excited passion. Hamlet does not hunger to do; rather, he thinks he ought to do. Consequently, his sense of moral obligation is a weaker driving force than his passion. Hamlet himself seems subconsciously aware of this; his self-reproaches mention his inability to *feel* his wrongs, as well as his inability to do anything about them. This realization is just as pronounced in the final soliloquy when Hamlet compares himself with soldiers who are willing to die for reasons far less important than his. On the other hand, the killing of Polonius is done when Hamlet is addressing his mother in terms of high acrimony, a moment when we can easily imagine his feelings to be running strong (as is amply demonstrated when all his pent-up emotions are spoken later in the same scene).

We may say of the Prince, then, that he is a man capable of bursts of passion which give him strength while they last. But these passionate moments do not last, and bereft of the drive they give him, Hamlet must fall back on a sense of duty, a sense of duty which ought to be sufficient but is not. He is a man capable of earthly valor, earthly nobility, earthly decision, on various occasions, but only when moved by earthly motives— and not the highest kind of earthly motives. The deed which he must do above all else, however, has no such motivation. It has been commanded by a higher power.

It promises no earthly rewards. It is a mission of justice in the eyes of other than those of this world, a task of setting wrongs right; we might almost say an *angelic* mission, and it is this work he is unable to accomplish because the driving impetus that can come only from his angelic nature is insufficient. There is consequently a struggle between the two natures in Hamlet, not the struggle of the higher nature to subdue and control the lower one, but of the higher nature to move the lower one to action, to arouse it to deeds worthier than worldly ones, rather than permit it to rouse itself here and there with smaller things of only incidental value or no value at all. But if a word of extenuation may be said in this connection, I might quote Ruskin's dictum that imperfection is more characteristic of higher aims than of lower ones. It is the simpler thing which is more perfectly done, for the very evident reason that it is well within one's powers and easily accomplished. We can truthfully say that where Hamlet fails he fails as an angel; where he succeeds he succeeds as a man.

Now, I realize many will disagree with me on this. They will say that Hamlet's mission was not the angelic thing I make it out to be; that all he had to do was to chastise the King, a thing Laertes does without a moment's hesitation, and which demonstrates conclusively that Hamlet could have done it just as easily had he only gotten around to doing it. Where is the exalted action or goal I am talking about? This indeed brings me to the heart of the tragedy, as I conceive it, and I would like to begin by seeing very clearly certain aspects of this contrast between Hamlet and Laertes. It is one worth examining. The obvious similarity of the situations in which they find themselves cannot escape us even if we were to read an outline of the play. Each man has a father murdered. Each feels called upon to avenge the murder. We see how Hamlet goes about it. How different is the bold and decisive manner of Laertes when, after hearing the news of his father's death, he bursts in upon

Claudius:

> O thou vile King,
> Give me my father!
> . . . .
> How came he dead? I'll not be juggled with.
> To Hell, allegiance! Vows, to the blackest devil!
> Conscience and grace, to the profoundest pit!
> I dare damnation. To this point I stand,
> That both the worlds I give to negligence.
> Let come what comes, only I'll be revenged
> Most throughly for my father.

Compare this with either of Hamlet's soliloquies wherein he meditates upon his father murdered and his mother debauched while he, their son, does nothing. There is no doubt that Shakespeare intended this contrast to be clearly noted. Far from having to be prodded into action, Laertes seems as if nothing on earth could restrain him. His language, his threats are intemperate to the point of being treasonable, and all this to the King who has had no part in the death of Polonius. Much may be said of misdirected rage and its dangers. However we may excuse it when it comes on the spur of the moment, Laertes has had all the time it took to travel from France to Denmark to get control over himself. He has no wish to control himself. Rage is his natural and only recourse, and all else is rudely thrust aside. "To Hell, allegiance!" "I dare damnation." The highest duties, in this life and the next, are dismissed because his father has been killed, he does not know by whom. There is, by his very words, no sense of duty at all. It is purely personal feeling that guides Laertes, if we may use the term "guides" in connection with so turbulent a nature. Where Hamlet may alternately possess and lack a conformity between personal feeling and sense of duty, Laertes is entirely taken over by the former. Eternal damnation itself is an unimportant consideration compared with the all-consuming fire of his rage. Such a man is capable of anything when aroused. He adopts a course which passion dictates and he holds to it even when passion has momentarily subsided.

This is essentially the difference between Hamlet and Laertes. When strong feeling subsides in Hamlet, the likelihood of what he might do (good or bad) subsides with it. But the cold, calculating way that Laertes plots treachery against Hamlet is ample warrant that he, Laertes, undergoes no such alteration. The reason he does not is simply that there is nothing in his nature to temper strong passion while it is present, nor to supplant it when it has abated. His character is fundamentally a smaller and simpler one, a character easily filled with one impulse and whose very emptiness insures an uninterrupted continuance of that impulse after the sharpness has worn off. What else is there for him to dwell upon? He can no more forget his father's death than Hamlet seems to be able to remember his. This simple fact taken by itself would predispose us in favor of Laertes if what it made him stoop to did not enable us to penetrate a little more deeply. We cannot pardon Laertes on the probability that the King has given him the worst possible version of Hamlet's slaying of Polonius. Treachery was not repaid with treachery, but was called to an honorable account. Laertes does not impress us as a particularly deceitful person. Once wrought up, however, he is capable of anything and his deceit is a natural consequence. He who is not in the habit of scheming and lying and pretending becomes something less than himself in executing what was supposedly an honorable duty. There is this about courage which is purely of the manly, or physical kind: that it is often capable of doing what higher motives seem incapable of; that it looks neither before nor after, but concentrates exclusively on the thing to be done and does it with dispatch. I say *purely* physical courage, and not physical courage alloyed with and under the influence of a different kind of courage. In its elemental state it is brave, it is cruel, it is savage and treacherous, and only a nobler quality can make it anything better. It is, in the very strictest sense of the words, the courage of the lion. It is not to be condemned in man, but neither is it to be trusted. Of all the counsel it will ever listen to (if it can be got to listen at all), it will hear the most wily and devilish, being a peculiarly apt prey to such things. When it is calmed it is calmed only by promise of future satisfaction, and with a willing ear it will listen to the most abominable stratagems and conspiracies as the means of securing it.

And why not? Its view is short, its analysis simple in the extreme, its impelling power to act irresistible. Is it any wonder that such a nature as that of Laertes banishes all considerations, all delay—or rather does not even need to banish them since they never occur to him in the first place—in marked contrast to the more complicated Hamlet? I have said Hamlet is an idealist, and I meant it in the sense that he has been accustomed to dwell in loftier and rosier realms than his present surroundings can match. We are first introduced to him when he has been awakened from this dream and has seen the world for what it truly is. The result is a sickening disillusionment and his prime impulse is to escape. But this impulse is the reaction to what we may call a passive suffering. He is scarcely capable of accepting the world to which his eyes have suddenly been opened, but the problem is nevertheless a simple choice between accepting and rejecting. It is a case of living or dying. Life would merely *happen* to him or *not happen* to him. He need take no active part in that life, even though floating with the stream might itself be painful enough. He might even withdraw into himself, sanctuarize his existence, and so avoid the world as much as possible; in fact, many of the early scenes in the play suggest he has already begun to do this. He is aloof and alone although none of the other characters gives us any indication that this has always been his way. This aloneness continues even through his companionship with Horatio, his one and only friend. What happiness he might have derived from such an existence had he the chance to continue it uninterrupted is difficult to say. Technically, we must pronounce him maladjusted. But the fact is that he must foresake even this retirement, re-enter the world and perform a horrible duty, the manner and means of performing it to be determined by him. The difficulties that lie in his way are insignificant indeed when compared with the soul-sensitivity which causes him to shrink and flinch at every turn as he appears on this sterile promontory in the first place. He must now embrace the life he loathes, for how else can he do vengeance upon the King except through careful laying of plans, great circumspection, and attention to all the things he would banish from his mind? His turning away from these things results from the fact that his angel nature is more subconsciously desirous of the joys it longs for than consciously willing to undertake the repulsive duties imposed upon it.

In the ideal person these two awarenesses in the angel soul are perfectly balanced. Duty may be no more attractive, but it is more readily undertaken. That is why Hamlet must not be seen as an ideally perfect man, even though he possesses a vast amount of the ideal. He is a tragic hero, not a triumphant one. In my analysis of him so far I have been careful, and I think correct, to see him as weak rather than strong. The play is not a success story; if it were we might very well expect the Prince to go calmly and evenly about the task imposed upon him, never flinching, never sidetracking, and only thwarted when circumstances block him beyond his ability to cope with them. But this does not happen, and the reason it does not is because of the presence of a higher, though imperfectly balanced, nature in Hamlet. It is one not visible in Laertes, and while it may render Hamlet less capable of acting in a given situation, it nevertheless puts him closer to what the ideal man should be. The error of thinking otherwise arises primarily from expecting a higher nature to reveal itself only in perfections. It is far more common for such a nature to give evidence of itself by imperfections, and by imperfections I do not necessarily mean a falling short from higher goals than those which the average man sets for himself in life. I am concerned with actions that lesser men are quite capable of doing, but which pose greater problems for greater men. This is not always the case, but there are so many instances of it that we can say the tendency is invariably present. Many a poet whose soul soars near heaven finds it impossible to put up with the drudgery of ordinary work which a less imaginative man does without difficulty. Many a soldier who has fought on the far-flung battlefields of the globe finds it difficult to adjust himself to the lesser experiences of civilian life. In a thousand different ways man is beset with difficulties in seeking to acclimate the vastness or meanness of his nature with the vastness or meanness of some object. If this be true in things relating only to everyday life it is infinitely more so when the angel soul, which is present in every man and the desires of which are never less than heavenly, is exiled into a world beneath it. Some men are more sensitive to this than others, and in precise ratio to their sensitivity are they rendered less fit to take their place in worldly existence—*unless* that heavenly desire, which is a desire for reward, be accompanied by a sense of duty, which is a desire to deserve. Then we have the ideal man whose minutest act is far greater than any act of the man who performs easily because he fits in readily. Earthly adjustment, not moral duty, smooths his path. The more exalted the nature of man, the less satisfied he becomes with pettiness, meanness, treachery, disloyalty. If that exalted nature is susceptible to spiritual pride, its original revulsion at the ways of others may soon be replaced with a consuming pleasure at the consciousness of its own superiority. If it is realistically honest, it will be conscious of its own faults as well as those of the world. It will also be conscious of virtues that exist elsewhere despite the obvious vices that seem to cloud them. Hamlet must be charged with the failure to see whatever virtues may exist in those about him, but the reason he fails is because the revulsion of his sensitive soul is stronger than his willingness to seek out the not quite so apparent goodnesses in this stale and unprofitable world. Not even his mission of justice can bring him to enter right into the affairs of this life with a ready and practical hand, with the result that existent virtues which might ease his state of mind go unseen. But this fault which is chargeable to Hamlet is one frequently met with among earthly nobility and those who desire the "finer things in life," as well as its parallel virtue among those who avoid the world for worthier reasons. Among the elect and the aspiring in life, how many have been truly willing to undertake disagreeable work; or if they have been willing, how many have gone about it for the sake of the work itself and not simply to amass money, ease, fame, all of which are only lower forms of the "escape" Hamlet desired for himself? And among the honestly pious it is certainly the hour of solitude that is more spiritually pleasing than that of mingling with the outer world. This is not said in any disparaging tone. The world is a dangerous and unrewarding place with right and wrong very closely intermingled. To become too indiscriminately a part of it is perilous as well as contrary to higher inclination. It may have to be done, but it is done with reticence and with considerations that may well prove to be a worldly disadvantage. The angelic nature does not render a man incapable, but the disillusionment and distaste that nature can experience renders earthly tasks doubly difficult. The more earthy are often more efficient, but it is the efficiency of Laertes.

All of this comes dangerously close to putting into a simple formula something which is immeasurably great and subject to infinite variations and graduations. My only purpose is to direct our view of Prince Hamlet along the proper roads, not to limit it in any way. I do not believe that anyone will ever say quite enough about Shakespeare, but enough can be said to clarify to a large extent this one character in which so many men can see themselves. No man is a perfect ideal and no man is completely without some shred of the ideal. As long as all are somewhere between the two extremes Hamlet reflects both failure to reach the height and dissatisfaction with the depth. But, conceding this to be so of everyone, not all dramatic types necessarily include this phase of existence as part of the character portrayal. For the sake of convenience, then, even though the basest and best characters may be said to possess varying degrees of bad and good in them (and so are variables on the Hamlet-type), let us turn to a few other Shakespearian creations and consider them as if they were different types. Hamlet may be seen more clearly if we note in what way he resembles and in what way he differs from characters who are somewhat like him.

Brutus is an idealist, a man of noble nature. Like Hamlet, he is faced with a terrible task. He must slay Caesar in order to save his beloved Rome from the tyranny of one-man rule. It is certainly not as easy for him to come to the decision at the beginning, as easy, say, as it is for those who act from base motives such as Cassius and Casca. They make up their minds with a readiness and decisiveness impossible to Brutus. Yes, the reader may say, but Brutus was loved by Caesar; the other two were not. It is more difficult to slay one you love, even in a high cause, than one you hate. True, but the personal love between Brutus and Caesar is part of the higher nature of Brutus. Cassius and Casca did not love Caesar, mainly because they are incapable of really loving anyone; and a nobler nature that will love and inspire love forms an attachment that may well impede a grim task, even though it be a highminded one. Furthermore, from Brutus's own words, it is the fact that Caesar has no personal demerits rather than Brutus's personal attachment to him that causes this mental struggle over consenting to do the deed. Both Cassius and Casca can see this as easily as Brutus can, or could see if their envious and cynical outlook did not blind them. But no one would contend that they are better men than Brutus because all three are faced with the same material task—the killing of Caesar—and the other two come to an immediate decision where Brutus hesitates. The one simple act is a much vaster thing for Brutus than it is for the others, vaster and more difficult because Brutus is the "noblest Roman of them all."

We can pursue this a little further. It is Brutus who actually blunders with regard to the consequences of their plan. Out of his noble and trusting soul he refuses to kill Mark Antony. The more worldly-wise Cassius knows better but Brutus refuses to follow his advice. And it is Antony who brings about the conspirators' downfall. From the inception of the plan through its execution and final consequences, which of them might have achieved more by contemplating less; and which, by dreaming of all, achieved nothing? The parallel contrast between the noble Brutus and the wise Cassius forcefully illustrates a difference between nobility and sagacity. The two are not mutually exclusive by any means, but as I said with respect to Hamlet there is always the tendency toward this strange dichotomy. There is little doubt that the higher quality is less efficient without the aid of the lower, or that the lower is misdirected when not guided by the higher.

But Brutus is not Hamlet. After the understandable difficulty of coming to the painful decision, Brutus does not hesitate or go astray. His mind does not wander off into other things, but he goes through with his task at the earliest opportunity. And he does it even though his decision could not be reached without strong arguments against it, whereas Hamlet's decision is obvious. I do not contend the two men are the same, nor that their tasks are exactly parallel. But on this point let me cite something of tremendous importance: Brutus is not disillusioned until very late in the play and after he has slain Caesar. Hamlet is disillusioned early, before his task even begins. The famous quarrel scene between Brutus and Cassius has an importance frequently overlooked. Brutus has made the tragic mistake of supposing his associates to be guided by the same noble motives he was himself guided by. They were not! Cassius, his closest co-conspirator, the one who had pretended so highly in the beginning, what is he now in the eyes of Brutus? What are all the rest but something less than what they once appeared to be, who stabbed "in envy of great Caesar," and not because they "loved Rome more"? Yes, Brutus acted surely and with determination, but only on the false assumption that the world was a better place than it actually was. He did not see the world as an unweeded garden with things rank in nature possessing it. There was only one weed and if that were uprooted the entire garden might once again be the perfect thing he imagined it could be. But suppose he *did* know better. Suppose he did see the danger to be anticipated from Mark Antony and his loyalty to Caesar. Suppose he did see the conspirators as something less promising than the saviors and guardians of their nation's liberty. What if his wife had killed herself before, not after the undertaking was launched—as Ophelia's defection comes while Hamlet is still plotting against the King? Would Brutus's resolution then have been so certain and so swift?

This hypothetical pre-disillusionment would, it might be said, complicate the *decision* of Brutus, not the acting upon it once the decision had been made. And Brutus would certainly have to be pardoned for not being able to come to this decision if he were aware of even graver arguments against it than those he is able to see. There are no such arguments in Hamlet's mind. He knows the thing ought to be done, yet he does not do it. Here again we must conjecture as to what might have happened had more been known. However, let those who would insist that the difficulties of Brutus are simply the difficulties of deciding what to do, and that once his decision is made there is no further hesitation —let those, I say, remember that the most moving expressions of Brutus's tormented soul come *after* his decision is arrived at and not before. "It *must* be by his death," Brutus affirms, and goes on to add "and for my part I know no personal cause to spurn at him, but for the general." Later he says,

O Conspiracy,
Shamest thou to show thy dangerous brow by night,
When evils are most free? Oh, then by day
Where wilt thou find a cavern dark enough
To mask thy monstrous visage? Seek none, Conspiracy—
Hide it in smiles and affability.
For if thou path, thy native semblance on,
Not Erebus itself were dim enough
To hide thee from prevention.

These thoughts are continual with Brutus after he has reached his decision, yet before he has any reason to doubt that the assassination of Caesar will produce the desired results.

But, alas,
Caesar must bleed for it!
When his boy has fallen asleep Brutus says:
Enjoy the honey-heavy dew of slumber.
Thou has no figures nor no fantasies
Which busy care draws in the brains of men,
Therefore thou sleep'st so sound.

Through the whole passage that follows in which he speaks to his wife who has wondered about his walking alone at night, the tenor of his talk clearly reflects the painful unwillingness in spite of which he must do what has to be done. "You are my true and honourable wife," he tells Portia, "as dear to me as are the ruddy drops that visit my sad heart." Granted Brutus's love for Caesar and Hamlet's hatred of Claudius as only one of the many dissimilarities and variables that render the comparison of the two men little more than conjecture, we may still hazard a number of things that will serve to bring Hamlet's problem into bolder relief. The question is a general one which Shakespeare often poses in specific instances of the idealistic character and his unfitness for the world as it is. This unfitness of Hamlet may be compared with that of Brutus, a different kind be it admitted; and the antithetical fitness of Laertes may be compared with the same quality in Cassius, which also has its specific variations.

Hamlet's eyes are wide open; he sees all for what it is, even a little worse than it is. But he sees from the heights of the ideal and is vexed with what he sees. Brutus's eyes are almost shut; he sees all for better than it is. He too sees from idealistic heights, but sees only other heights which can be assured by removing the only threat within his view. Included in all the differences that result from this, there is this fine psychological distinction that renders their temperaments so far apart: Brutus believes a near perfect state of things will result from his action; Hamlet has no such illusion. Rome, which Brutus loves more than his own life, has been glorious in the past and it will be glorious in the future. Denmark oppresses Hamlet with its ribaldries and carouses, its plottings and wickedness. It is a prison, he says; the world has many confines, wards, and dungeons, Denmark being one of the worst. Nor does he entertain the slightest conviction that Denmark or his own life will be the happier when he avenges his father. What to Brutus is a fruitful mission, a means of achieving a shining goal, is to Hamlet a disagreeable penance in a dungeon of gloom. Hamlet's very vision is a spiritual block which only a stronger nature than his can overcome. Brutus's blindness is a spiritual impetus. Hamlet shrinks from his task. Brutus undertakes it too willingly.

This distinction is quite as true of the worldly counterparts of both men. Laertes is blind where Hamlet sees and, like Brutus, moves too swiftly. But the blindness of

Laertes is not that of Brutus. Laertes sees only depths where Brutus sees heights, and Laertes is not farseeing even among them. Cassius also sees only depths, but he sees far and wide among them; he is circumspect, cautious, always anticipating consequences and ready to shape his plans accordingly. There is, among the four men, an almost perfect scale of deterrent feelings, arising through knowledge and up to high-mindedness. Laertes, who is the least seeing and who is without lofty purpose, is the most impulsive of all. His actions are instantaneous and utterly without plan of any kind. Cassius is next. He is not so ready to act as Laertes, because he lays careful plans and always looks before he leaps. It is noteworthy that, regarding Cassius and Brutus—the one who has vision and the one who has idealism—vision is less of a deterrent to decisive action than is the latter. The ever cautious and careful Cassius has made up his mind and proceeded while Brutus must still agonize with himself. Yet this slowness to act cannot be traced to even the slightest trace of cowardice on the part of Brutus. Just prior to the assassination of Caesar before the Capitol, it is Cassius, not Brutus, who grows momentarily panicky and thinks their purpose is discovered.

Hamlet is the slowest of all. Vision to him is not mere caution as it is in Cassius, but, united with the elevation of idealism, is disillusionment. Cassius sees only obstacles before him. Hamlet sees objects of revulsion beneath him. Nor is his idealism a goal before him, as it is with the comparatively unseeing Brutus, but something behind him, a height from which he has had to descend to regions thoroughly unbeautiful.

Some would explain Hamlet's delay, and his not pursuing the wisest course, as due to a kind of youthful bewilderment; that he was, after all, a young and inexperienced prince setting out to catch someone much older, wilier, and far more resourceful than he. This, of course, contains some truth if by the word *youth* we mean inexperience, but we must always return to the inescapable question as to whether Hamlet was anxious to do his duty or anxious to avoid it. Was he baffled by the task, or was he revolted by it? The unfitness that may be ascribed to the Prince is something far deeper than a mere lack of apprenticeship in bringing villains to justice. Here again, let us compare *Hamlet* with some other plays with regard to this notion of unfitness in the good person and see if we can further isolate the peculiar kind found in the character Hamlet—often resembling, yet never the same as that of so many other Shakespearian creations.

King Lear and *Othello* are largely tragedies where the good suffer because, being good, they are too unsuspicious of the wicked. Lear, for all the criticism scholars have heaped upon him for his treatment of Cordelia, would have been far more fortunate had he been of a suspicious nature; he would have discerned, not only the deceit of Goneril and Regan, but the true love of Cordelia as well. He is too fundamentally honest and believes other people mean what they say. Too ready to accept appearances as indicative of the inner whole, he never probes beneath the surface. He cannot divine trickery, and when his world is shaken one day as a result, he lashes out in the wrong direction—rewards the evil and punishes the good. But even the tragedy that develops from this might have been averted, temporarily at least, if, despite Lear's inability to suspect falsity, Cordelia were capable of practicing it. A situation bred of the hypocrisy of the other two sisters brings two good people to an estrangement that only further hypocrisy can ease. When Goneril and Regan are pressed by their father to say how much they love him, they pretend such a deep love and paint it in such glowing colors that any honest statement of daughterly affection on the part of Cordelia is bound to appear flat and empty by comparison. She realizes this and when given her turn to speak she can simply reply, "Nothing, my lord." The impact of the whole evil atmosphere upon one who sees it in its true light is summed up in that one significant word, "Nothing." Cordelia's honesty has no place in such an atmosphere and she would rather say nothing than speak honestly. Vision, if we may use the term with respect to so brief an incident, she certainly has, and with it comes that familiar-recurring reluctance to do or say at all. It is true that she does speak out honestly in the following lines, but only when pressed twice to do so, and the dreadful misunderstanding between her and her father is in no way allayed by it. Here we have the predicament in which two good people are put in a false position, and the reluctance of the one (which must be pardoned) and the impulsiveness of the other (which must be condemned) brings undeserved tragedy to both. Neither can meet the situation forced upon each, but a too ready willingness to meet it on the part of Lear precipitates the misunderstanding into a catastrophic error.

Gloucester and Othello commit more or less the same mistake. As with Lear and Brutus, so with them. They realize too late how wrong they have been. Unlike Brutus, Lear and Gloucester do not go through the slightest bit of quandary and delay. They act impulsively upon what, if appearances are correct, are high motives. Othello takes a longer time to act, but only because Iago's villainy is a deliberately protracted process and takes a longer time to work on its victim. We may pose the question of them as we did of Brutus: suppose the entire truth had been revealed to them in advance; would they have been any more reluctant to act? It is a moot question, but I believe they would have acted just as swiftly against the actual villains as against the supposed ones. There is something of the Laertes readiness in them, without his tendency to stoop to treachery. They are good men, noble, just, even though one does not think of them as idealists. They lack a certain self-control; their feelings are too easily aroused and they commit dire acts; they do not pause to think, in fact they are not thinkers at all in any real sense of the word. Their margin of possible error is a very broad one indeed. In a situation wherein they know the truth they are ideal performers. Everywhere else they are in danger from their very willingness to perform. They are good men, but by no means above the world in which they live. They may be said to be outside wickedness—or wickedness outside of them—rather than above it, and as a result they have no experience with its workings or manifestations. They do not know enough about it to recognize it or combat it and are consequently helpless when unexpectedly confronted with it. That is the extent of their blindness. If they were to know evil their vision would, of course, be more extensive, but only in so far as they know evil. Such vision would be of practical advantage to them. It would guard against mistaking evil for good. But it is difficult to imagine them seeing anything further than this or occupying themselves with loftier contemplations. None of them has any notions whatever of an ideal world, as Brutus has, nor of the limitless nature of man, as Hamlet has. It is, therefore, easy to understand that such vision as Lear and Othello might be capable of, could they see further, would in no way be a deterrent to action on their part. They do not contemplate vast achievements wherein the presence of evil would militate against success, nor are they accustomed to dwell in golden realms where evil sickens and disgusts. Their noble natures may indeed be above those of the villains in their midst, *without*, however, being on a higher plain altogether. They *do* know evil exists. They may to some extent be pardoned for not recognizing evil when it arises from an unexpected quarter—in Gloucester's son, in Lear's two daughters, in Othello's trusted friend and confidant— but this failure to detect it, while arguing a noble and trusting nature, is not the result of a belief that no evil exists anywhere. There is at least one instance in which each of these three is brought face to face with what he believes to be evil, but the effect is not as devastating as it is upon Brutus and Hamlet. Gloucester is informed his son Edgar plots his father's death. Lear infers from Cordelia's words that she loves him no more than she is required to. Othello finds, or believes he finds his officer Cassio remiss while on duty. Yet, as dismaying as these things are, they do not cause the tragic upheavals in the bosoms of the principals as are caused in the other two more idealistic characters. Nor can it be argued that these incidents are less serious than Gertrude's hasty remarriage or the itching palm of Cassius. The difference of reaction lies not so much in the comparative seriousness of the deeds committed, as it does in the difference of those who view them. Evil seen simply as wrongdoing is one thing. Evil as a muddy blot upon an almost divine perfection is quite another. For Cassius to sell and mart his offices for gold to undeservers may not appear to be a very serious crime as the world goes. But Brutus cannot forget that the hand that did this also stabbed great Caesar, supposedly in a daring plunge toward a heartfelt ideal.

Three of these men possess goodness, but it is the goodness of the world in which they live. The goodness of both Brutus and Hamlet is otherworldly, the only difference being that the former does not realize this and believes the present world can be shaped to the heart's noblest desires. Such innocence of knowledge on the part of Brutus is largely responsible for his mild-mannered demeanor. For he seems ever mild and gentle to us, even when his heart is suffering at the thought of his having to kill Caesar. However, when knowledge finally does reach him and this state of innocence is swept away, strange moods and feelings surge up in Brutus. Many a reader must be surprised at the discordant and angry snappings of the noblest Roman of them all in the quarrel scene with Cassius. It seems so unlike him. Neither the pressure of imminent battle nor the death of his wife can entirely explain it. Shakespeare scarcely gives us this protracted scene to inform us that the pressure of events is beginning to tell on Brutus. It is rather the tragic collapse of the ideal right then and there, not in the crude sense of the conspiracy having been defeated (since it has not been defeated yet; the battle of Philippi has not been fought at this point), but because it is rotting away with the baser elements that compose it. It is this that so vexes the feelings of Brutus and it is in this scene that he shows most like Hamlet. The opening of the eyes upon inner ugliness and rot precipitates in each man a burst of emotional bitterness. The innocence of knowledge evaporates, but the innocence of feeling is intensified and soured into violent and even foolish acrimony, from which it generally subsides into a melancholy indifference. Brutus might have thus subsided were it not for the fact he is already committed to a course which is afoot. Hamlet, in a similar state of disillusionment, has to formulate one.

Hamlet is like Brutus, Lear, and Othello, in that all four men are unfit for their arenas of life by virtue of an innate goodness. But Hamlet differs radically from the others in that their unfitness arises basically from insufficient knowledge. The Prince possesses the knowledge they lack, and possesses it to the point of complete realization. Again and again this is made abundantly clear as his judgment of character after character proves to be the correct one. Where is Hamlet mistaken about another character? He does indeed commit one important misjudgment which I wish to speak about later, but nowhere is he guilty of the painful misconceptions that so tragically afflict these others with respect to those about them. Hamlet's knowledge is so complete and so accurate that one does not wonder at the cynicism into which he so often falls. To his credit we can say that, while many of his utterances are undeniably cynical, we do not classify him or even think of him as a cynic. His is too broad a nature to be categorized under the title of confirmed cynic, even though the world to him is a sterile promontory. His very shrinking from such a world is but an indication he can never resign himself to it in the form of the perennial misanthrope. Whatever souring of youthful sensitivity may have taken place within him, that sensitivity is still there in something like the original virtue from whence it arose, and it is this virtue, this innocence of feeling, which is both the saving grace of the Prince as a man and the spiritual encumbrance which impedes the work he must perform.

I have already pointed out that a more harmonious balance between elevated sentiment and a strength acquired of personal inclination, would have enabled him to act more easily. We do find both in Hamlet, but they are there at different times and he fluctuates as he is under the spell of one and then the other. That is why we see his temperament undergoing the many alterations during the course of the play. But, as we shall see, whatever strong feelings of the moment cause him to speak and act with vigor, these are sporadic outbursts utterly discordant with the nobler quality he usually exhibits. They come in isolated instances. It is Hamlet's spiritual nature which is the more prevalent and it prevails in that peculiarly disadvantageous way that makes virtue something of a fault. Any virtuous quality may prove to be in some sense harmful in the absence of other virtues. This happens when a situation occurs in which other virtues are sorely needed. Before the death of his father Hamlet's sensitivity of spirit no doubt served him well and guarded him against temptations toward uglier things. But in the play itself he is expected to be a strong man of justice, a thing quite different from that of a poetic or sensitive soul. His dominating quality is there instead, a virtue still, but useless for what is demanded of him, quite opposed to it in fact.

Had Hamlet's dominating quality been generosity he would have been tempted to forgive the King rather than punish him. But there is not the slightest indication of his ever relenting in his feelings toward Claudius. Had it been loyalty he might be expected to have serious qualms about regicide. Though the notion of regicide no doubt contributes to the difficulty of the task, Hamlet never specifically mentions it. Any quality in the Prince that could be directly expended on the King would be a likely form of substitute behavior, a method of treatment which would take the place of that which duty commands. An indifferent quality would simply occupy Hamlet elsewhere and make him indifferent. But the one he actually does possess does not soften him toward Claudius, nor does it render him indifferent; it actually intensifies his detestation. Though he blows hot and cold during the course of the play, his changes are never the result of any softening toward the King either through indifference or through any kind of warming up to him, however mild.

This would bear a little pondering. If anything, Hamlet's feeling of revulsion toward Claudius would seem to be an added incentive to punish him. If duty becomes easier when assisted by personal inclination, as I said it does, then it would seem to follow that the righteous slaying of the King would be made easier by this personal distaste which becomes stronger as the play proceeds. However, if we examine it more closely we can see why it would have the very opposite effect. Keeping in mind all I have said regarding Hamlet's sense of a lost perfection, a descent from heights to a world that sickens him, let us bear in mind that this feeling is brought on by no one so much as the King himself. It is Claudius who personifies everything Hamlet loathes. Polonius is an annoyance. Ophelia hurts him but his love remains unabated. There is certainly no reason to think her repulsive in his eyes. His mother becomes corrupt in his view, but this is solely because of her relationship with the King. Rosencrantz and Guildenstern become false friends, but this again stems from the King; and though I have previously listed disappointed friendship as a harsh thing, it is to be questioned how much this would have affected Hamlet if all else were perfect. Laertes seems not to have bothered Hamlet prior to their clash at the grave of Ophelia, and there is no reason to suppose they ever had much to do with each other or that Laertes was important enough to Hamlet to upset him to any great extent. It is the King who is

> A murderer and a villain,
> . . . a vice of kings,
> A cutpurse of the empire and the rule,
> That from a shelf the precious diadem stole
> And put it in his pocket!

Ironically, this is the very person the Prince cannot bring himself to kill, though he has every justification for doing so. And the reason why he cannot is because this revulsion to the King and his own weakness compound each other, not cancel or assist each other. A nature that recoils from the deliberate execution of the King is not aided by a similar recoiling from the King's own person. Unpleasantness is a mild word here, but if we can sharpen its meaning to the point where it can be understood to cause an almost suicidal gloom we have Hamlet's state of mind at the outset of the play. And the King is the evil tree from which this grows. It is gloom, revulsion, abhorrence. It is not a burning animosity. It is the feeling that was there first and it produces in Hamlet a desire to escape, not a desire to injure in return. As bitter as he is toward his uncle at the beginning of the play he says nothing of wanting to harm him. The desire for escape is there first and it is strongly rooted in him before he learns this man is the murderer of his father, and he, Hamlet, must avenge it. Admittedly, his reaction to the ghost's revelation is passionate and intense, but in the long run this revelation does little more than confirm, or provide defensible reasons for, what Hamlet has already felt. His original feeling is so overpowering that even the murder of his father can scarcely make it more so. It is not that he is indifferent to his father's death at the hands of the hated uncle, but that he has been too acutely pained prior to hearing of of it. His soul has not been numbed, exactly, but flooded with suffering already, and he would be free of the guilty Claudius and free of the life of which Claudius is the central and ruling part. This feeling, while it has existed only for the comparatively short time since his father's death (at the earliest), is so naturally rooted to Hamlet's nature as we have seen it that it can scarcely be supplanted by a new feeling of vengeance.

Hamlet would not have easily slain anyone if he had to do it with calm deliberation. Undoubtedly he would have been tempted to put it off even as he puts off the slaying of Claudius, simply because it would be difficult for him to bring himself to do it. And putting it off would make it prey on his mind with all the torment of a duty not fulfilled. If one thing did not recall this duty to mind, something else would. The recalling would never be a pleasant experience. But where the torment of such unwelcome reminders is compounded by another torment, the result is doubled. Quite subconsciously Hamlet builds up in his mind an association, one with the other. He can never separate them because circumstances have bound them inextricably; the thought of duty brings with it thoughts of the King, and vice versa. Hamlet desires to escape in two different connections, each of which binds him not only to itself but to the other as well. It is significant that, of the two incidents which demonstrate to him how inescapable it all is—the actor who feels passion but in a fiction, and the soldiers who are going off to fight and die under Fortinbras—the first has reference to personal feeling, and the second to a cold sense of duty. Each strikes Hamlet in a very apt way, showing him on one occasion what he ought to feel and on another what he ought to do. We must see each attitude in isolation in order to appreciate what they amount to in conjunction.

There is something to be said for Goethe's interpretation of Hamlet as representing "the effects of a great action laid upon a soul unfit for the performance of it."[6] But, while I believe the German writer's interpretation to be somewhere in the right neighborhood, it is both incomplete and devoid of significance. It concentrates exclusively on the Prince's quailing before a harsh undertaking, and so concludes (logically enough, if other factors are overlooked) that Hamlet is simply not strong enough to bear his burden. Goethe's further remark, " . . . an oaktree planted in a costly jar, which should have borne only pleasant flowers in its bosom; the roots expand, the jar is shivered" makes the slaying of Claudius a virtual impossibility for Hamlet's insufficient powers. This only sounds like what I have attempted to show. In addition to omitting any reference to the instances of Hamlet's violence and brutality as well as his very evident courage, it does not properly evaluate Hamlet's own attitude toward his failure. To this we must always return. It is an honest admission of guilt, of inexcusable weakness, of failure to accomplish what is by no means impossible. The difficulties, both external to Hamlet as well as internal, are there just as they are present to every living man in one form or another. No man behaves in all times and places with the facility of bestial instinct; the very height of his nature is a partial repository for the drives and motivation by which he must act, and every rise in the scale toward perfection has its moderating or sedative effect upon stimuli which are purely emotional. Or, if a man does behave with the instinct of the beast, this in turn becomes his problem—one of controlling the ready impulse rather than dispelling the facile inaction. As we shall see, Hamlet is faced with this problem as well as the other. Shakespeare takes great pains to indicate that when Hamlet's vehemence is aroused it does not cooperate with the gentler nature, but replaces it. It works of its own accord, and then it is that Hamlet becomes like Laertes. It demonstrates why

Hamlet could, in a moment, do anything Laertes can do; but in the long run it is Hamlet who has the greater and more difficult task to perform, and the very difficulty with which he performs it elevates him, while the simplicity with which Laertes performs his lowers him. One is the angel-man. The other is mere man.

IV

ANGEL IN PURGATORY

In studying any character in literature we must examine all and only the material in the work which in any way relates to him. A good artist chooses his material judiciously and exhibits his character clearly so that the reader may see deeply into the portrayal from many angles and points of view. But the artist is necessarily limited in portraying character, and there is always the danger of rendering a false impression of character if one phase or one sequence of events is concentrated upon too strongly. We are apt to think of such a character in terms only of the thing dwelled upon and in no other connection. This is not always the case, even where we see only one side to a particular character, but sometimes it is.

Let me illustrate. Viola is portrayed chiefly as a girl in love and we think of her in no other connection, unless, perhaps, that of a devoted sister. In a certain strict sense this is an incomplete picture of Viola. As far as the picture goes it is complete and thorough because we see her in so many different moods and situations, but we know perfectly well there must be more to her than that. And it is just because we do know this that we do not feel that since Shakespeare limits his portrayal of Viola to the circumstances surrounding her love for Duke Orsino he gives us a false impression of her. The mere fact that we know it is simply the story of her love life, that the selection of this is *so obviously* a selection, prevents our leaping to any false conclusions about the rest of her character. We think of Viola only as a lover, but we are not in danger of thinking her unduly a lover and nothing else. What we do not know of her we do not pretend to know. But where a character portrayal goes deeper than this there is danger that the artist may emphasize certain things—and thereby give them a prominence they ought not to have—or that the reader may draw false inferences by weighing this very prominence against what appear to be less important considerations. How can a man's soul be portrayed, for instance, unless we know what he thinks about? And how can the artist exhibit his character's thoughts without conveying the idea he is a thinker? If the character *is* a thinker there is no special problem. But suppose he is no more thoughtful or moody than the next person, and yet it is necessary for us to see him continually soliloquizing, debating with himself, pondering, and so on. What then? The difficulty cannot be solved (though it may help some) by scrutinizing what the character thinks about and deciding his "thinker" status by the depth or shallowness of his thoughts. Hamlet thinks upon some very deep subjects, and the temptation has existed in some quarters to regard him as a poet or philosopher. This need not be disputed, though it may do some harm to my contention that Hamlet represents all of us; I tried to demonstrate this in the first place by showing that, while Hamlet's problems are singular and in a sense peculiar, they can nevertheless be taken as representative of the problems all of us have to face. This representativeness would be lessened, if not altogether destroyed, if it could be shown that Hamlet himself is unusual. As far as the general nature of man is concerned, as well as the problems that face man in life, I attempted to show that Hamlet's character has some application to all of us. But this application is an all-inclusive one and within it there are certainly many uncommon types which, in whatever way they are uncommon, cannot be said to be representative. To prove Hamlet is no such unusual type leaves me with the alternatives of proving either that Hamlet is not a philosopher or that the rest of us are.

Instead of beginning with a too ready and exact answer to this question, I would rather examine Hamlet once again, this time relative to his usualness or unusualness and whether he does or does not fit into the world in which he lives. Dr. Huhner,[7] in proving Hamlet was not insane, stresses among many good points the very pertinent one that nobody in the play regarded Hamlet insane *before* he saw the ghost. The same thing might be said regarding any unusual characteristic ascribed to him. There is no evidence that anyone else ever thought Hamlet in any way unusual prior to the death of his father, and while many do regard his behavior as a little odd during the play (and some of them think him insane), none of them considers him a person who thinks overmuch. Horatio's brief remark in the graveyard scene, "T'were to consider too curiously to consider so," can hardly be taken as an awareness of the Prince's general tendency to thinking, even by one who knows him as intimately as Horatio does. And when Laertes and Polonius both attempt to persuade Ophelia against him neither of them mentions anything of his moodiness or his proclivity to troubling thoughts. It is logical to suppose they would have mentioned this if Hamlet were given to it and they were aware of it. It would make much better sense than the ridiculous notion that Hamlet is too young to know his own mind and is therefore not to be trusted in his vows of love. Insofar as Polonius and Laertes mention Hamlet's personal character in addition to the supposedly real reason for their opposition (the fact that Hamlet is a prince and therefore not free to choose his own wife), their remarks are notably at variance with what we know of Hamlet's character. And it is pertinent that they speak to Ophelia two months after the death of his father and one month after the remarriage of his mother, time enough for them to have observed changes in his deportment which these two events would presumably have brought about. His mother, his uncle, Ophelia, Horatio —none of them express any opinion of Hamlet as one spending much time by himself thinking.

It might be objected that others would be poor judges of how much time any person spends thinking, since nothing is as private as a person's thoughts. This may be generally true, but it is hardly likely that the behavior of the Prince of Denmark would escape the notice of those about him in the court. They might not know the extent of his thoughts, but they would certainly recognize some marks of the thinker or philosopher in him, just as people come to recognize a man of prayer even when he takes deliberate pains not to make a show of it. Ophelia's opinion of Hamlet,

> The courtier's, soldier's, scholar's, eye, tongue, sword —
> The expectancy and rose of the fair state,
> The glass of fashion and the mold of form,
> The observed of all observers —

reveals Hamlet as a kind of paragon of all the virtues of

an aristocratic gentleman of the day, but says nothing of any qualities that might set him outside or above society. And she as well as the others speaks of any strange behavior as something quite different from what she has always known him to be. So that, as far as we are able to judge of Hamlet before his father's death (in the eyes of those around him), he must have appeared normal without being average or mediocre.

Now, there is no doubt that all this refers to Hamlet before the action of the play, which is not the Hamlet we know. He has undoubtedly changed; he must certainly think more now than he did before, having more to think about. But this change or this new behavior, even as time goes on (definitely fixed as four months at the performance of the play within the play), is not spoken of as "thinking." It is considered madness by some; the King considers it dangerous. If for the sake of argument we grant that Hamlet emerges a different man during the course of the play and those in the court have not yet come to recognize the change for what it actually is, what other evidence is there that he is essentially the brooding type? Hamlet's thinking is done chiefly in the famous four soliloquies, and in all of them his thought is related, directly or indirectly, to the action of the play; it is never thought for its own sake. It is the perfectly understandable thought of a man faced with difficulties that put his willingness to a severe test. The notion that Hamlet's procrastination is because of the fact that he is a "thinker" rather than a "doer" arises from overemphasizing the soliloquies and seeing the best known one as entirely extraneous to the events before and after. If that were so we would be correct in saying that Hamlet's tendency to indulge in reflective meditations interferes with his ability to act decisively.

It is true that he is unable to act and this inability is certainly related to thought. I have already spoken of his actionless thought as opposed to the thoughtless action of Laertes, and that the longer Hamlet has to think about doing something the more difficult it becomes for him to do it. But we must understand that this thinking is the result, not the cause of the delay. To say he thinks, and therefore cannot act—this is to state it backwards. He cannot act; therefore he thinks. If I may return to the example of the man on the high diving board, it is the dread of the act which first stops him rather than "thinking too precisely" which comes later. Thinking about it may indeed minister to the original fear and increase it, but that is a very different thing from saying that thought of itself comes first and acts as a preventive. The first time we hear Hamlet express a wish to avoid his mission is at the close of the scene in which he speaks with his father's spirit. He has had little or no chance to think about it at this point. But his calm and usual self has returned and this, rather than long periods of thought, brings on the desire to avoid what he is faced with. Seen in this way Hamlet is not unusual. He cannot be designated as a special kind of man or thought of in connection with what belongs basically to one category only. The man on the diving board concentrates on what he shrinks from, while the man in the easy chair is perfectly relaxed. But the difference is in the situations, not in the men. To offer the comment that another man might dive immediately would only reopen what I have discussed in the previous chapter as to different men having to perform identical acts. For now let us simply bear in mind that an unusual situation creates an unusual man. Hamlet thinks because he is preoccupied and not because he is primarily a man of thought.

However, when we come to the question of Hamlet's sensitive soul, or what I have called his "angelic nature," it is not so easy to prove that he possesses such a thing, or that if he does he still maintains some kind of identity with all men. We can demonstrate that he is not by nature an exhaustive thinker and that no one in the play regards him as one. But what I have said about his soul is not substantiated by the opinions of those who know him. There is not a bit of evidence that the others in the play (with one notable exception which will be commented on in another chapter) have ever descried this part of him, or that, praiseworthy as Ophelia and Fortinbras find him, his excellences are any more than worldly ones. I have spoken of him as possessing something of the ideal. Nobody in the play does. Nor do I think any reader who finds Hamlet an attractive personality, has in mind the courtier, soldier, scholar of Ophelia's eye, the "glass of fashion and the mold of form, the observed of all observers," or anything else of this sort. It is something very different. We get no chance to see Hamlet as a soldier or a scholar, and almost none as a courtier, but even if we did and even if Hamlet were perfect as all three, I doubt if there would be the slightest hint of the angelic nature we do see in the man who cannot perform his duty. Horatio, the only one in the play who knows all, comes closest to expressing it when he says,

> Now cracks a noble heart. Good night, sweet Prince,
> And flights of angels sing thee to thy rest!

It is briefly said, but it is much for Horatio to say, and the character of Horatio, which Shakespeare takes great pains to make clear, is the last one to make such a statement out of mere sentiment.

There is a striking dissimilarity between our opinion of Hamlet and the opinions of those around him. Except Horatio, if any of these others were to write a character study of the Prince it would be a far cry from what many a scholar has had to say. The combined opinion of the former must be given due weight because there are so many of them, they are so varied in character themselves, and they stand in such different relationships to Hamlet that taken together they have the opportunity to observe him under every conceivable circumstance. If we see Hamlet as strange, aloof, sensitive, suicidal, we must appear to be dismissing an overwhelming mass of evidence to the contrary. This disagreement of interpretation would be logical enough—at least we would readily understand it—if we could show that no one in the play is close enough to Hamlet to observe what he is really like. The plain fact is, however, that many of them are close enough. The filial relationship to Gertrude, the love relationship to Ophelia, the long-standing friendship with Rosencrantz and Guildenstern, the fact that he is the nephew of Claudius and that he is heir-apparent and Polonius chief counsellor to the King, are certainly sufficient bases for understanding Hamlet somewhere, somehow. Yet none of these know him as we know him. His mother, his beloved Ophelia, his friends Rosencrantz and Guildenstern — what we see in Hamlet has escaped all of them. The side they do see cannot be denied, but it is the all-but-hidden side that primarily interests those who study the play. This failure to see any more than the worldly attributes of the Prince cannot be explained away by the shallow retort that it is his ghost-commanded mission which is secret, not his character. His character is established in the play prior to the appearance of the ghost to him. Hamlet did not become the character he is only after the first visit from his dead father, even though the reaction to the ghost's message would serve to make this character more manifest to us. In other words, admitting that the reader knows Hamlet far more intimately than anyone in the play does (with the possible inclusion of Horatio), it is significant that his angelic nature—if angelic nature he has—escapes them all.

A Shakespearian character should be studied in the light of what he reveals about himself and of what others reveal about him. But there are notable instances in which the other characters fail to reveal. Nobody, not even Roderigo, sees Iago as he really is. This is not because everyone else in *Othello* is stupid, but because Iago is clever. Not only is he clever, but he is able to put up such a show of honesty that the "honest Iago" in the mouths of all is a commentary on his very deceitfulness.

But Hamlet, far from being consciously deceptive, seeks vainly to make himself understood; the basis on which he has always been acceptable to people in the past is no longer a true kinship—if it ever was in the first place—though it is the only basis on which they will meet him now. The revelation of this to the reader is a very gradual and subtle process which begins in the very first scene in which Hamlet appears. It may not be suspected the first time the scene is read, so prominent are the facts of the elder Hamlet's death and his surviving wife's remarriage; at least it may not be fully appreciated. But the unfolding of the many things which follow serve to render far more meaningful the Prince's first agonized outburst when alone: "How weary, stale, flat, and unprofitable seem to me the uses of this world!" We have already seen this introductory portion as chiefly emphasizing a lack of compassion for one in sorrow. It is more than this. If Hamlet's associates will not bend some kind of attention upon him at a time like this, when will they? It makes very little difference that certain individuals close to him are absent at the moment and the company on hand is largely made up of those whose relationship to him is never more than distantly cordial. Hamlet's loneliness is not brought on by what takes place in this scene the manner and matter of which is typical rather than unique. If we have any doubts about this we have only to read the rest of the play in connection with it to see how amply all is borne out.

Polonius and Laertes are indifferent to Hamlet in this scene; their only concern is Laertes' returning to France and securing the King's permission to do it. The King and Queen attempt to persuade Hamlet to spend no more time mourning his dead father, but this is not until the more important things have been attended to and Claudius can, as it were, turn to matters of less moment. The Prince is an afterthought. He might not even be that except for the fact that his persistence in wearing black is an uncomfortable reminder to Gertrude and Claudius.

None of the four people who know Hamlet best is in any state of mind to be noticing (or if noticing, admitting) anything like a superior nature in the man Hamlet.

In the very next scene Laertes and Polonius try to persuade Ophelia against Hamlet, but their reasons do not agree with one another. Laertes thinks Hamlet too young to know his own mind; Polonius thinks Hamlet's vows "mere implorators of unholy suits." And Polonius scolds Ophelia for speaking as a "green girl," inexperienced in such things. Is it not strange that Laertes thinks Hamlet too young too realize the gravity of his princely position in connection with his love life, whereas Polonius thinks Ophelia old enough to know better? Ophelia can hardly be older than Hamlet even if we disregard the gravedigger's chronology. This rendering of disagreeing reasons by Polonius and Laertes betrays a strange and unaccountable opposition to Hamlet, particularly since there is no good reason why Ophelia should not marry the Prince and they not think it an honor. The Queen, whatever her faults, can be believed when she says at the grave of Ophelia

> I hoped thou shouldst have been my Hamlet's wife,
> I thought thy bride bed to have decked, sweet maid,
> And not have strewed thy grave.

If she, the Queen of Denmark, saw no objection to the marriage, it is not likely these other two could have seen any. The very tenor of all their advice, despite the fact that it contains good reasons as to why Ophelia should exercise care in how she receives Hamlet's protestations of love, indicates a peculiar, an almost unwarranted antagonism. Polonius is especially peremptory. He does not show the slightest trace of understanding or even the desire to understand anything beautiful in this budding love between his daughter and the Prince of Denmark, or what possibility it may have of coming to happy fulfillment. He scoffs at it and commands that it immediately cease. He is certain, or pretends to be certain, that Hamlet has dishonorable intentions and nothing else.

POL. What is it between you? Give me up the truth.
OPH. He hath, my lord, of late made many tenders
Of his affection to me.
POL. Affection! Pooh! You speak like a green girl,
Unsifted in such perilous circumstance.
Do you believe his tenders, as you call them?
OPH. I do not know, my lord, what I should think.
POL. Marry, I'll teach you. Think yourself a baby
That you have ta'en these tenders for true pay,
Which are not sterling. Tender yourself more dearly,
Or—not to crack the wind of the poor phrase,
Running it thus—you'll tender me a fool.
OPH. My lord, he hath importuned me with love
In honorable fashion.
POL. Aye, fashion you may call it. Go to, go to.
OPH. And hath given countenance to his speech, my lord,
With almost all the holy vows of Heaven.
POL. Aye, springes to catch woodcocks. I do know,
When the blood burns, how prodigal the soul
Lends the tongue vows. These blazes, daughter,
Giving more light than heat, extinct in both,
Even in their promise as it is a-making,
You must not take for fire.

Hamlet and Ophelia may or may not have committed indiscretions, but Polonius can hardly have adequate grounds at this point for thinking they have. Just prior to the passage quoted he tells Ophelia he has heard she has been "most free and bounteous" of her audience to Hamlet. This may mean anything, and we do not know who told it to Polonius nor how much his informant knew. But he is evidently speaking to his daughter about it for the first time, and though he must seek information from her as to what is between them and whether she believes him and so forth he scoffs crankily whenever Ophelia in any way defends Hamlet's love. He who knows nothing knows everything. "My lord, he hath importuned me with love in honorable fashion," she tells her father, and "hath given countenance to his speech, my lord, with almost all the holy vows of Heaven." We cannot think Ophelia is lying when she says this. This has been the way in which Hamlet has addressed his love to her. Can Polonius suggest a more appropriate or honorable approach? Can he or can we think Hamlet a smirking fornicator whose holy vows are nothing but snares to catch fools as Polonius insists? Yet Ophelia's perfectly reasonable belief that Hamlet means what he says is brushed aside and she is forbidden to have anything more to do with him. A very pious attitude on the part of Polonius, but rather ready to detect the worst, and somewhat incongruous in a man who apparently sees nothing wrong with the marriage of Gertrude and Claudius. However, such is the cynicism with which age sometimes views the beautiful ideals youth shapes for itself, a cynicism perhaps more often right than wrong in its avowals of sin in the young, but far more wrong than right when it insists sin is intended from the very beginning. Polonius's notions of Hamlet's designs are utterly inconsistent with the character of the Prince and with his own approval of the royal marriage.

Even in Laertes' attitude there is a hint of hypocrisy. After Ophelia has listened patiently to Laertes' advice as to how careful she should be of her purity, and she replies

> good my brother,
> Do not, as some ungracious pastors do,
> Show me the steep and thorny way to Heaven
> Whilst, like a puffed and reckless libertine,
> Himself the primrose path of dalliance treads
> And recks not his own rede.

Laertes' terse "Oh, fear not. I stay too long." has all the marks of an uncomfortably brief rejoinder. As lengthy as he has been in discussing his sister's uncautious attitude toward the dangers to her chastity, he would quickly end further discussion now that his own sins are being broached. Ophelia must have some reason for saying what she does, over and above any mere petulance she may feel for the moment, since later in the play Laertes does prove to be a creature of uncontrollable passion. Much or little may be read into his ardent desire to return to France.

On the whole, Polonius and Laertes seem able to see only the worst side of Hamlet here, and nothing further in the play would indicate they have ever seen or ever wish to see anything particularly good about him. Laertes' becoming friends with Hamlet at the moment of their death near the end of the play, sincere and noble though it be, does not alter nor modify what his views have been all along. And Polonius who suspects his daughter, and who later sends Reynaldo to sniff out his own son's possible backslidings in France, has an ever ready eye for faults, not virtues, and is an inveterate snooper in his desire to find them out. However capable he may be as a counsellor to the King, in other ways he is so easily thrown off the track, so conspicuously in error as to Hamlet's madness, that we cannot credit him with shrewd powers of observation nor be surprised that his continual probings for evil fail to detect what is noble and good.

But what of Ophelia? I have all along insisted the love between Ophelia and Hamlet sincere on both sides, and if they are sincerely in love it is strange she has no insight into his noble soul. She is not prejudiced against him in any wise, nor, even though she obeys her father without a murmur, does she show the slightest inclination to concur in his opinions. On the contrary, when Hamlet seems to be so unfeeling toward her in Act III, Sc. i, she speaks of herself as "of ladies most deject and wretched, that sucked the honey of his music vows." Now, this love will bear some examining. I say their love is sincere as opposed to its being pretended or shallow. But I will not go so far as to say it is a perfect mating of two hearts, or even that it is as deep as we might expect sincere love to be. Nor did it blossom in circumstances that were ideal for its growth. By adverse circumstances, of course, I am not referring merely to the opposition of Ophelia's father and brother. Many a Shakespearian heroine has gone counter to the wishes of parents or leaped over other impediments thrown in her way, which impediments have often determined her choice and actually hastened love's culmination where an ideal situation might have delayed it. But in these cases the lovers are ordinarily occupied with love alone; their actions may be thwarted, but not their feelings. Hamlet, however, is distracted by many things which he must ponder upon and which act as a diversion from the love he might otherwise have freely felt for Ophelia. This is no insincerity on Hamlet's part; the fact that love is not the main plot of the play is the result of its not being the only, or even the main thing Hamlet has to think about. It is for this reason that Hamlet says comparatively little about his frustrated love, a fact which has led some to believe he did not really love Ophelia or he would have thought more on it, as we would expect an unhappy Shakespearian lover to do. As a matter of fact, Hamlet's vexations are so many that we can make the same argument against any of his interrupted affections. Their very number reduces the amount of specific attention he can give to each, and if we confine ourselves to a comparison of any one of them with the total amount of Hamlet's thinking and brooding, the ratio will be small and very misleading. Taken together they more than fill his mind and cause him to wish for that eternal escape.

Hamlet's feeling for Ophelia, far from being shallow or pretended as some have thought, is a strong and impassioned love which is amply demonstrated on three separate occasions. The first is the rather strange behavior related by Ophelia to her father in Act II, Sc. i; the second is the acrimonious flare-up which immediately follows the To-be-or-not-to-be soliloquy in Act III, Sc. i, which I have already discussed; and the third comes in Hamlet's outburst at Ophelia's grave. This last has been called mere show by some commentators, a boast of love in front of a crowd of spectators and prompted by a desire not to be outdone by Laertes. I will discuss this more fully later on, but I will say just for now that this explanation is very unlikely since there is little reason to regard Hamlet as an exhibitionist, then or at any other time. And what is the reason for Hamlet's behavior in the first instance I mention, that related by Ophelia in Act II, Sc. i? She bursts in upon her father, all excited about something:

OPH. Oh, my lord, my lord, I have been so affrighted!
POL. With what, i' the name of God?
OPH. My lord, as I was sewing in my closet,
        Lord Hamlet, with his doublet all unbraced,
        No hat upon his head, his stockings fouled,
        Ungartered and down-gyved to his ankle,
        Pale as his shirt, his knees knocking each other,
        And with a look so piteous in purport
        As if he had been loosed out of Hell
        To speak of horrors, he comes before me.

Is this exhibitionism too? It can hardly be a purposed show of madness (which we know Hamlet resorts to later), for it bears no similarity to the pretended madness Hamlet adopts in front of Polonius. In addition, the King already knows of this supposed madness. Polonius, upon hearing this account from Ophelia, decides that Hamlet is mad on account of unrequited love and determines to go right to the King and tell him. In the very next scene he comes to the King with this explanation, but before he arrives the King has already been speaking with Rosencrantz and Guildenstern about Hamlet's transformation and his "being so much from the understanding of himself." Moreover, when Polonius arrives and says he knows the reason why Hamlet is mad, neither the King nor the Queen betrays any surprise; it is certainly not the first they have heard of it, even from Polonius.

Before this happens, however, Ophelia tells her father more about Hamlet's startling manner:

He took me by the wrist and held me hard.

> Then goes he to the length of all his arm,
> And with his other hand thus o'er his brow,
> He falls to such perusal of my face
> As he would draw it. Long stayed he so.
> At last, a little shaking of mine arm,
> And thrice his head thus waving up and down,
> He raised a sigh so piteous and profound
> As it did seem to shatter all his bulk
> And end his being. That done, he lets me go.
> And with his head over his shoulder turned,
> He seemed to find his way without his eyes;
> For out o' doors he went without their helps,
> And to the last bended their light on me.

What can this unprecedented deportment mean but that Hamlet sincerely loves Ophelia and fears that he is about to lose her? His sigh "so piteous and profound as it did seem to shatter all his bulk and end his being" is certainly a manifestation of extreme sadness, the kind of feeling which Hamlet is neither capable nor desirous of counterfeiting. We begin to understand the reason for it in the next few lines when Polonius asks his daughter if she has given him any hard words of late, and she replies:

> No, my good lord, but, as you did command,
> I did repel his letters and denied
> His access to me.

We must remember that it is only in the scene just previous to this one that Hamlet has learned for the first time of the mission that is to be such an oppressive load upon his mind and heart. Undoubtedly some time has elapsed because Ophelia speaks of repelling his letters and denying his access, and since Polonius's command that she do this was given her on the same day that Hamlet talked with the ghost, it is safe to assume some while has passed. But in this interim, whatever its duration, Hamlet sent letters to her and attempted to see her. What must have been the effect on him when she—now, of all times, and without a word of explanation—rebuffed him? We can imagine it only if we realize what prompted him to love her in the first place. Hamlet fell in love with Ophelia because of the attraction of her tender beauty to which he would naturally turn in the collapse of all else about his shoulders. This can be conjectured from the fact that this love is of recent date and not a long and slowly maturing one. Both Polonius and Ophelia speak of it as something that has taken place "of late." Hamlet has been home from Wittenberg since something less than two months, and nothing is said of his having written to her prior to his arrival; nor is it likely Polonius and Laertes would have waited until the courting had gone on for some time before speaking against it. This would mean that Hamlet began to make the many tenders of his affection, only after the death of his father and very probably after the remarriage of his mother. His attraction to Ophelia must certainly have been the more poignant because of these soul-shattering events, but by the same token we cannot think of the sensitive youth who suffered them an ideal lover in his tragic state of mind. Hamlet began to love this beautiful girl because he needed her, or because he needed what she dimly symbolized to his suffering soul. It is not the materialist who idealises physical beauty, but the man who dwells in the things of the spirit. Wandering in an inferno of desolation, Hamlet sees Ophelia in a light of lone-angel brightness. She is the only being who attracts him, the only direction in which he may turn with some hope of love and spiritual consolation.

When we consider that he must have seen Ophelia in other days but that it is only "of late" he has been making love to her, and when we consider the easily inferred state of mind which prompted this love, we cannot wonder at its being rather sudden and certainly with words of "sweet breath composed," as Ophelia says it has been. Why does he love her all at once? Can she suspect the real reason? Polonius and Laertes certainly do not, and there is at least some logic in the concern (though not their certainty) over Hamlet paying a too sudden and too ardent attention to Ophelia and she yielding herself too quickly to him. Moreover, the more we imagine the feelings of Hamlet in his dark desolate world and his crying need for the love of Ophelia, the more likely we may imagine his courtship of her to have been secret. Without implying anything dishonorable, we may see it all as a love so hidden from others as to excite some suspicion. It is no ordinary love affair. Hamlet's desire for privacy with Ophelia is not the usual desire of lovers to be alone in order that they may open their hearts to each other without the benefit of an audience. Most lovers do desire such moments to themselves, but at other times they are perfectly willing, still in their relationship as lovers, to join the society of those about them and enter into the normal amenities of everyday life. Hamlet could not do this with Ophelia. To him she is the one sacred thing in this "unweeded garden," a kind of sanctuary or shrine that would lose its very blessedness if transformed into merely another easily fitting part of the court life he loathes. We cannot imagine Hamlet entering into the carousing and merry-making which the King decrees, in any event. Much less can we imagine him dancing with Ophelia or in any way partaking with her of the general mood of jollity that seems to prevail with everyone else. Both before and after the King has declared that all be joy despite the recent death of the elder Hamlet, the Prince's love of Ophelia is precious only insofar as it is removed from everything else about him. He would be loath to connect Ophelia's father with it in any way, recoiling from any discussion of his intentions with Polonius who, to him, plays all too prominent a part in this dusty milieu. Imagine his love as the beautiful thing Hamlet hoped it would be, and then note the irritating contrast of Polonius's know-it-all "Affection! Pooh! You speak like a green girl, unsifted in such perilous circumstance." The eyes of a world far more worldly than that of Hamlet can be expected to read it in that light. Even if Hamlet himself were to explain his feeling for Ophelia as eloquently as his tongue were capable, Polonius, far from being any more understanding, would be vexed to the point of exasperation. His world and Hamlet's are so far apart that the two men neither speak the same language nor think the same thoughts.

Without condoning the bullishness of Polonius we may plead some excuse for his failure to appreciate what he knew nothing about. At least he is a little wiser now when he admits he was mistaken in supposing Hamlet's intentions frivolous:

> I am sorry that with better heed and judgment
> I had not quoted him. I feared he did but trifle
> And meant to wreck thee, but beshrew my jealousy!
> By Heaven, it is as proper to our age
> To cast beyond ourselves in our opinions
> As it is common for the younger sort
> To lack discretion.

But this acknowledgment that Hamlet was in fact in love with Ophelia can hardly be taken as a full realization of Hamlet's feelings. The Prince has already been behaving in some way that leads Polonius to think him mad, and any plausible explanation is likely to be seized upon. He says:

> This is the very ecstasy of love,
> Whose violent property for does itself
> And leads the will to desperate undertakings
> As oft as any passion under heaven
> That does afflict our natures.

This is a reason for Hamlet's insanity (Hamlet is *not* insane), not a recognition of love unrequited. Polonius is nearer the truth than he was ever before because there is now something that can be interpreted only as evidence of love, but he still blunders. And it is not difficult to see why if we know the kind of person Polonius is. Shakespeare juxtaposes Ophelia's description of Hamlet directly on top of Polonius's exhaustive instructions to Reynaldo about spying on Laertes in Paris. He tells Reynaldo to accuse Laertes secretly to his friends in order to see if they reciprocate with stories of the young man's wild behavior, which Reynaldo can in turn relay to Polonius. Passing over the question as to how despicable is this sort of thing, we may easily conclude as to how Polonius busies himself and where his mind works. Never is he capable of imagining anything beautiful, nor willing to look for it.

Now, is Ophelia of the same mind as that of her father and of her brother; or does she enter into full and sweet accord with Hamlet? Despite her protests as to her lover's sincerity she betrays no emotion, not even a trace of disappointment, when her father orders her to have nothing more to do with Hamlet, but says simply, "I shall obey, my lord." She repels his letters and denies him her company. How different is the decision of Juliet, of Desdemona (who anticipates her father's opposition and leaps over it), of Jessica, or of even more passive women such as Perdita and Miranda! Ophelia's willingness to comply with her father's wishes, while it bespeaks a dutiful daughter, is strangely at variance with the filial disobedience of these others who were truly in love. Yet she cannot have remained wholly unmoved by Hamlet's solicitations, even after her father's stern prohibition. True, her emotion in Act III, Sc. i, seems occasioned more by her belief that Hamlet is insane than by any acknowledged disappointment in love; but it is precisely because she does have some personal feeling for him—call it love or something less—that her grief over his supposed insanity is the more poignant. She would not have been the most deject and wretched of ladies merely because of the mental collapse of one to whom she had ever been indifferent, regardless of how perfect a man he had been before. And while she never admits to having loved him, even after he has departed and she is by herself in this later scene, her language is not that of an indifferent or unmoved lady. The conversation she and Hamlet have just been through—his "I did love you once," and her reply, "Indeed, my lord, you made me believe so"; and again, to his "I loved you not," her reply, "I was the more deceived"—is not the language of a lady who has not made at least some progress toward loving. It is true that this conversation is being overheard, as Ophelia knows, but she has not been instructed to say these things nor would they exactly fit anything Polonius might in the past have instructed her to say. If anything, she would be more guarded, not more forward, in unveiling herself to Hamlet while she knows her father is listening. Furthermore, when Ophelia goes mad (Act IV, Sc. v) her distracted singing refers about equally to the death of her father and her having been played false in love. Whatever she may have failed to say or do that might be expected of a girl in love, is more than compensated for now by a mind demented that runs over things which must have occupied it for some time.

We may say of Ophelia that she is somewhere between the state of mind of Polonius and Laertes on one side, and accord with Hamlet on the other. The opinions she expresses on several occasions are highly laudatory of the Prince, in contrast to anything we ever hear from her father and brother. On the other hand, never does she evince anything like a complete understanding of the man who loves her. Her catalogue of his virtues which I have previously quoted represents the way he must often have appeared to her eyes before he began to woo her, not an unimportant thing in the eyes of any lady, and which undoubtedly persisted after he did begin to press his love. This is the Hamlet she remembers, and once again it is *not* the one we know. It is not even the Hamlet that loved her.

Differences like these, however slight, are incalculable handicaps to young lovers. It is not a case of minor differences which we might expect to find among even the most perfectly harmonious pair, such as Hamlet liking music and she not caring for it, or Ophelia preferring to walk in the afternoon while Hamlet would rather read poetry. We have seen the almost heavenly longing with which Hamlet must have opened his heart to her. What response can she have made if, in her highly emotional state after Hamlet seems to have rudely cast her off, she remembers him as nothing more than a proper gentleman? That she was flattered by his attentions, or quickened by them, or pleased, we can grant. She sucked the honey of his music vows. But was it not rather Hamlet who had need of drawing sweetness and not supplying it for another? If Ophelia could not divine the true anguish of Hamlet's soul when he made love to her, why could she not have done so in that touching instance when he stood before her and fell to such perusal of her face "as he would draw it," and looked on her as something lost to him in the future? She did not. She was not moved to the tiniest feeling of tenderness. She was frightened! Hamlet's true soul, which may have been unrecognizable under the guise of a lover, is suddenly stripped bare and he is the proper gentleman no longer. It terrifies Ophelia. She does not know what to make of it. She runs breathless to her father. Is there no significance in this? Polonius, the one whom the suffering Hamlet would keep his love clear of, the one whom we have just seen giving his sneaking instructions to Reynaldo, he is the one to whom Ophelia flies when the soul of the loving Hamlet reveals itself.

It is true that Polonius is her father. But Ophelia explaining with girlish obedience that she has done as he commanded is not a lover who has ever reached anything like communion with the Prince whose actions appear so strange to her. This same lack of understanding is further revealed when she returns her gifts to him. The acrimonious explosion of Hamlet on this occasion surprises and overwhelms her mainly because she cannot see the reason for it. She has not the slightest intuition to recognize a mind vexed to the breaking point, and which actually does break when she comes to restore gifts that have been given while a sacred faith in love still burned. Again Hamlet acts from a sense of losing Ophelia, but while his manner is vastly different the second time it makes no more sense to Ophelia than did the first. He is "like sweet bells jangled, out of tune and harsh." He is "blasted with ecstasy."

In all the portrayal of Ophelia's character, however, she remains the sweet and attractive thing to us that she must have been to Hamlet. There are no obvious faults, no glaring defects which would prevent our being drawn to her. She is, in fact, one of Shakespeare's most subtle creations in this respect, for the dramatist intended us to find her thoroughly attractive and tender, even when she is shown to be devoid of the ideal with which Hamlet has attempted to endow her. A rose in the unweeded garden, she is too thoroughly ensconced in and domineered over by shabbier growths. Her very tenderness, though it matches Hamlet's sensitivity, has this essential difference: it is too soft, too easily guided into a baser world, too trusting. And it is because of this that the pair would be drawn to each other and at the same time mismatched. Each judges the other on the basis of the widely different world in which each one lives; Ophelia sees less in Hamlet than is really there, Hamlet credits Ophelia with more than she possesses. Their love story specifically demonstrates why Ophelia cannot be accepted as an adequate judge of Hamlet's character. It is the unhappy tale of a man more powerfully drawn to a woman than she is drawn to him, because he sees more than she does, even though the most important part of what he sees is illusory. Her beauty first attracted him. But he is forced to the conclusion that that beauty, allied with every other feminine grace of the purely material kind, constitutes her sole possession. It attracted because it suggested so much more. Rather than a catalogue of spiritual virtues to be exercised when occasion called for them, it suggested a beauty of spirit itself. But Hamlet, with the memory of his mother never absent from his thoughts, sees Ophelia, not as having committed any wrong, but so blighted by indifference to the sacredness of love as to class herself with the evil rather than the good. As yet she is uncorrupted. But her simple resignation to spiritual nonentity clashes violently with her physical beauty, and the reaction is violent in Hamlet when he realizes it. Even if we make allowances for emotional hyperbole we miss the entire point of what Hamlet says when he makes this discovery:

> . . . if you be honest and fair, your honesty should admit no discourse to your beauty.
> . . . the power of beauty will sooner transform honesty from what it is to a bawd than the force of honesty can translate beauty into his likeness. This was sometime a paradox, but now the time gives it proof.

Only by dismissing the heavenly-minded nature of Hamlet, as revealed time and again, can we assume that he is referring here to an illicit love between himself and Ophelia, or that he concludes that since Ophelia has abandoned their love she must be a bawd.

The very directness with which Hamlet speaks proves only that he loves her still. He sees her here before his eyes as he has always seen her. But the lack of that something else which belongs with the power of beauty makes Ophelia, not Hamlet, "like sweet bells jangled, out of tune and harsh."

Lastly, there are Rosencrantz and Guildenstern. We know that part of the reason why they fail to see Hamlet as we see him lies in the fact that they have been away, that they have been summoned back, not by Hamlet, but by the King; that they are spoken to first by the King, in league with his thoughts, and consequently to some extent set on against Hamlet. They are not overly clever in their assignment to spy upon him. Though Hamlet is entirely unsuspicious at first, he very quickly sees through the game they are playing and never trusts them afterward. In Act II, Sc. ii, Hamlet divines the real purpose of their visit and forces them to admit it:

HAML. But in the beaten way of friendship, what make you at Elsinore?

ROS. To visit you, my lord, no other occasion.

HAML. Beggar that I am, I am even poor in thanks, but I thank you. And sure, dear friends, my thanks are too dear a halfpenny. Were you not sent for? Is it your own inclining? Is it a free visitation? Come, deal justly with me. Come, come. Nay, speak.

GUIL. What should we say, my lord?

HAML. Why, anything, but to the purpose. You were sent for, and there is a kind of confession in your looks which your modesties have not craft enough to color. I know the good King and Queen have sent for you.

ROS. To what end, my lord?

HAML. That you must teach me. But let me conjure you, by the rights of our fellowship, by the consonancy of our youth, by the obligation of our ever preserved love, and by what more dear a better proposer could charge you withal, be even and direct with me, whether you were sent for, or no.

ROS. (*Aside to* GUILDENSTERN) What say you?

HAML. (*Aside*) Nay, then, I have an eye of you. — If you love me, hold not off.

GUIL. My lord, we were sent for.

Now, it is pertinent that *after* this faltering admission by Rosencrantz and Guildenstern, Hamlet reveals to them in the most direct and open way, precisely what the nature of his problem is. Few things in the play give such an adequate and concise key to his character.

I will tell you why. So shall my anticipation prevent your discovery, and your secrecy to the King and Queen molt no feather. I have of late—but wherefore I know not—lost all my mirth, forgone all custom of exercises, and indeed it goes so heavily with my disposition that this goodly frame the earth seems to me a sterile promontory. This most excellent canopy, the air, look you, this brave o'erhanging firmament, this majestical roof fretted with golden fire—why, it appears no other thing to me than a foul and pestilent congregation of vapors.

This is a very close approximation of the first soliloquy in which Hamlet complains how weary, stale, flat and unprofitable seem to him all the uses of this world. Further:

What a piece of work is a man! How noble in reason! How infinite in faculty! In form and moving how express and admirable! In action how like an angel! In apprehension how like a god! The beauty of the world! The paragon of animals!

As I have pointed out in a previous chapter, this is an idealistic picture of the soul of man as we have seen it in Hamlet, a soul that cannot shrink itself to the narrow and sordid structures of the world. Why does Hamlet express himself so openly to these two, of all people? There is certainly no affinity, no mutual trust, that would urge him to do it. Furthermore, Hamlet has just caught them in what, to him, is a piece of dishonesty; they have admitted it only after being discovered.

First of all, Hamlet has just been through that silent scene with Ophelia previously alluded to, in which he gazes upon her so piteously and then leaves. Directly after this he has had to put up with Polonius's nonsensical and obvious probing to find out whether or not he is mad. Then come Rosencrantz and Guildernstern whom he greets at first with sincere welcome, but who shortly prove to be nothing more than spying emissaries from the King. The exasperation Hamlet feels at this point can easily be imagined, for his mind is preoccupied—as it has been from the beginning—with matters Rosencrantz and Guildernstern would never understand. Though these two are not particularly dense or slow-witted as the world goes, they are nevertheless part of the court they represent and to which they must repair with explanations of Hamlet's changed behavior. What would they or Polonius care for Hamlet's conception of man's soul or its exile in a world that stifles it? Court life is not concerned with questions of this sort. Yet here are Rosencrantz and Guildenstern come to seek answers. As in so many cases of this kind, the very question—if the two men were to ask it in so many words — is neither open nor broad enough, but restricts the answer to things readily comprehensible. Anything beyond the simple and the palpable does not answer what they are asking, but, in the strict sense of the word, eludes it. In a miserable intuition of the difference between his and their conception of reality, Hamlet understands all this. But he is provoked enough to make the truthful answer, knowing full well it will not be understood or even seriously commented upon. In a tone of high irony and contempt he says

> I will tell you why. So shall my anticipation prevent your discovery, and your secrecy to the King and Queen molt no feather.

This is as much as to say, very bluntly, "all right, I will tell you just what you want to know, and your secretly reporting it to the King and Queen will betray no confidences"; or, to put it a little more tersely, "O.K., O.K., here it all is; now go tell it to the King!" He is not humorously sarcastic as he mentions his gloomy state of mind or how wonderful is the nature of man. It is not good-humored fun at the expense of the other two. It is ironic, contemptuous, not in the sense that he means not what he says, but that he realizes he is delivering it to uncomprehending ears. Beginning in a tone of exasperated calm Hamlet warms a little to the spirit of what he is saying and then waxes wondrously eloquent where he begins with "What a piece of work is a man!" He becomes almost sincere, since the words themselves are so sincere, but with a sincerity that never quite smothers the irony with which he started out or the hopelessness of making himself understood. This is quite apparent from his insistence that what he says is so, though they by their smiling would not seem to agree with it. Why else would he be so attentive to everything about the other two, their looks, their smiles, their mannerisms, before and during the time he is speaking this singularly true speech?

The question may be raised, however, as to whether Hamlet is unable to make himself understood by Rosencrantz and Guildenstern, or is simply cautious about what he can allow to be conveyed back to the King. These two have come from Claudius, after all, and Hamlet knows they will report whatever he tells them. Is it not the vengeance upon Claudius which Hamlet must keep secret and which consequently makes him very guarded about what he reveals to others? It would be logical to think so if there were any evidence that this is on his mind and there were no evidence that it is not. But the very reverse is the case. Remember that this same scene ends with the appearance of the players, the impassioned performance by one of the players, and Hamlet's famous second soliloquy in which he plainly informs us that he has *not* been thinking about his father's murder or the mission of justice he should have been about. What he has told Rosencrantz and Guildernstern was not said for the purpose of concealing anything; it was not subterfuge because Hamlet soliloquizes in precisely the same vein when he is by himself.

Yet, as is so often the case, Hamlet's words sound pointless because they are unexpected and beyond the comprehension of those to whom they are addressed. If there be any doubt about this it is cleared up in the opening of the very next scene when Rosencrantz and Guildenstern repair to the King. Questioned about what they could learn of the Prince, they reply that they have been put off:

> ROS. He does confess he feels himself distracted,
> But from what cause he will by no means speak.
> GUIL. Nor do we find him forward to be sounded,
> But, with a crafty madness, keeps aloof
> When we would bring him on to some confession
> Of his true state.

If what Hamlet said was not a confession of his true state, what else was it? He was not keeping aloof. There was not the slightest evidence of "crafty madness" or that he was not "forward to be sounded." Guildenstern might think so because Hamlet detected the purpose of his and Rosencrantz's visit, and when they could make no sense of his answer they would naturally assume he was putting them off. But it is clearly they who fail to understand, not Hamlet who fails to speak truthfully. The irony with which the Prince addressed them was pertinent, to say the least, for nowhere do we find such evident demonstration of the incommunicability between him and those about him.

Claudius and Gertrude are intentionally deaf to the voice of conscience, and consequently just as intentionally blind to the true Hamlet who constitutes a living commentary on the sinfulness of their deeds. They, Polonius, Laertes, Ophelia, Rosencrantz and Guildenstern either fail or refuse to see the deeper Hamlet. It is equally plain that he is unable to reveal his true self to them. Despite his efforts to do so he is destined to be accepted as simply another person, a person with many merits no doubt, but not the man suffering anguish in the desolation of everyday life. In this respect he bears some comparison with Henry VI since neither man has any real desire to take part in the life and problems in which he finds himself. But Henry, for all the tragedy of his position, is at least spared relationship on a basis of what he is not. Hamlet is besieged with intimacies that are in fact not intimacies at all, but stale and sterile irritations.

Should we resurrect the possibility that Hamlet is a curiosity after all, far removed from all the people around him and therefore just as far from anyone who studies the play?

These others see nothing wrong with one another. They are apparently all quite normal to each other and well adjusted to the society in which they move. On the basis of this alone we might conclude Hamlet is wrong and the others right, since the preponderance of opinion is against him. I am not speaking now of Hamlet's being right or wrong with respect to the murder, which the others know nothing about, but of his individual soul-awareness which contrasts so markedly with the worldliness of those around him. This question might be settled by re-analyzing Hamlet's character in search of anything that could be construed as actually wrong, or by attempting to argue the merits of the question itself. Both would really come to the same thing. But a simpler, though less direct, means would be but to cite once more that universal appeal which the character of Hamlet has always had. He, indeed, has always been each one of us in his view of the world, his attitude toward duty, his relationship to those near him. Many who see themselves in Hamlet may not care entirely for my analysis or many of the terms I have used, but I believe their sympathies are as much with Hamlet as mine are. It is not my purpose to prove Hamlet right in everything he did, or failed to do. Yet I see him as essentially rightminded, and those others in the play who fail to understand him as wrongminded.

Admission of this is contained in the view held by some, that the court of Denmark is diseased and that certain key figures such as the King and Queen and Polonius illustrate this disease in a semi-symbolic way. This is to a certain extent true, of course, but it substitutes a pointless vagueness for what is abundantly clear. In what way is the court diseased? We know a murder has been committed by the reigning King, adultery by the Queen, in addition to a too quick forgetting of her precedent lord. We know the court errs in too readily acquiescing in the marriage between Gertrude and Claudius. But does this make the whole court diseased? Did the secret sins of the present King and Queen infect the entire court? And did the infection spread in the short time since the elder Hamlet's death? That there is corruption in the court is perfectly true, and it is just as true that Hamlet centers his feeling about this chiefly in the King. But it is difficult to see Laertes, Ophelia, Rosencrantz, and Guildenstern as particularly diseased people. Worldly they are, soulless, materialistic. But one feels that they, together with Polonius and others, would be the same regardless of the crimes of the King and Queen. Nor does the particular kind of worldliness which each exhibits belong to any specific time and place. Their types, as well as Hamlet's reaction to them, are too commonly met with to be identified with a corrupt court. The King and Queen are horribly conscience-stricken and wide-eyed when Hamlet succeeds in bringing them face to face with their sins, but these others have not sinned and Hamlet is not attempting any retribution or reformation among them. What they have done is to allow their souls to stifle away to the point where they fail to recognize that faculty when it manifests itself in someone else. Sensitivity of soul resides to some degree in all men, but it is a quality not readily observable. It is the most difficult thing to communicate to others and is often the least apparent. When it is so marked as to render a man actually different and consequently force his withdrawal from society, it is seldom recognized for what it is. Society does not use expressions like "sensitivity of soul." But when a man is readily accepted according to the mores of the society in which he moves, this quality, generic though it be, is completely overlooked. A careful study of Hamlet's relationship with those in the court shows that, although he has sore need of spiritual compatibility and although he speaks directly from his own soul, he is neither responded to nor understood.

When we are introduced to Hamlet it is at a time when this difference between the soulful one and the worldly many is widened to an unusual degree. But as the death of his father becomes a little more remote this separation contracts somewhat. It cannot shrink to whatever minor differences separated Hamlet from other people in the carefree days that are gone forever, but it can become smaller and a little more bearable. He can attempt to resume some kind of accord in the few restricted areas permitted by present circumstances. Even this is impossible. Where he feels most need of opening his heart—to Ophelia—he finds that no crushing and disillusioning sorrow inspires in her the need of something heavenly such as he seeks himself. But sorrow, the most certain thing in life, always has this effect. It enlarges the spiritual life within and reduces the acceptability of the material life without. The sufferer becomes the introvert, and though many kinds of opposites may attract, a discordance between introvert and extrovert can only repel. Hamlet can be known and loved only through self knowledge, and not by observations which are the communal property of society.

V

HORATIO

Literary analysis is sometimes at fault in seeing only tormented, complex or weak characters as dramatically interesting. Ordinarily they are the only really interesting creations, not only because they tend to be more human, but because the human soul itself is far more penetratingly revealed in failure and struggle than in easy conquest. We would rather follow the soul-searing tortures of Othello than a succession of calm and agreeable experiences of one who never knew anguish or frustration. If we hold fast to this general rule we are committed to an adverse opinion on the dramatic interest of the character of Horatio. Through all the soul-searching-ness of the play *Hamlet*, through all the tension and tragedy, Horatio moves with comparatively little emotion or upset, says little, faces no problems. To be aware of this much is to find him dull—oh, no doubt a good man and perhaps a fine friend in actual life, but not a character of any appealing interest in high drama.

I have long differed with this view of Horatio and have come to find him, next to Hamlet, among the most interesting characters in the play. I do not mean this in any obvious way, such as his being a striking contrast to the others which renders him conspicuous, or that he performs important dramatic functions such as serving as a foil to Hamlet. I am speaking of his character as such. It is a character frequently under-read, if not overlooked altogether, because of this foil-to-Hamlet designation which reduces Horatio to a kind of convenient hand-dial that turns Hamlet on and off for the audience's enlightenment and listening pleasure. Not only does this ignore Horatio's own individuality, but such a view leads to strange inconsistencies in the character of Hamlet himself. More than one writer has wondered the why and wherefore of the Prince's apparently deep friendship with this man of the court who seems to do nothing more than dog Hamlet's heels and listen to him speak. To mate them properly Hamlet must be reduced or Horatio expanded in some way. Failure to do one or the other leaves us with a situation that runs something like this: the Prince of Denmark, an unhappy and sensitive idealist who cannot stand contact with life and people, suddenly begins a warm friendship with a man whom he has known before, a rather colourless and silent character who, when he speaks, seems always to agree with the Prince; nothing ever really explains this friendship, except possibly that Horatio is so very agreeable whereas the others frequently do not see eye to eye with Hamlet. Such an opinion is untenable, unless, of course, it leads to the inevitable conclusion that all of Hamlet's idealism is a need for more yes-men. This reduces Hamlet far beneath what even a slighting estimate would be willing to allow. But such reduction would not be necessary if Horatio were seen in anything like the light in which Shakespeare intended him to appear, and we must see him by first ridding ourselves of the notion that Horatio is a mere crony or follower of the Prince. Hamlet's admiration alone, makes something more of his friend than that, and this admiration is hardly a false estimate of Horatio (as we shall see), nor can it be dismissed as a sentimental effusion prompted by Horatio's loyalty.

> For thou hast been
> As one in suffering all that suffers nothing,
> A man that fortune's buffets and rewards
> Hast ta'en with equal thanks. And blest are those
> Whose blood and judgment are so well commingled
> That they are not a pipe for fortune's finger
> To sound what stop she please.

Admittedly this is said at a time when, as we have seen, Hamlet has particular need of the strength of Horatio; but this need, though strongly felt, is not such as to unbalance Hamlet or cause him to utter half-hysterical exaggerations. On the contrary it is one of those moments frequently met with in real life when a very disconcerting weakness in ourselves makes us recognize more clearly the corresponding strength in someone else. Hamlet does not praise his friend here for any quality he can be shown not to have nor does it fail to square with what we see of Horatio elsewhere, even though it is the fullest commentary on Horatio's character which appears anywhere in the play. It is the strength and poise of Horatio, not his loyal friendship, of which Hamlet speaks. Consequently, if we should feel inclined to impute the Prince's attachment to Horatio to an unworthy fondness for whoever will accompany him and agree with his every remark, such imputation will not bear the scrutiny of precisely what Hamlet says. There is no reason to think Hamlet praises his friend simply because he is a friend, or that he fails to see him as he is—as, say, Bertram fails to see Parolles in *All's Well That Ends Well*. Hamlet says nothing as to Horatio's astuteness or cleverness or anything else which, if Hamlet be an egotist, could be translated to mean he likes Horatio only because Horatio likes him. On the contrary, he attributes virtues to his friend which are quite independent of any personal harmony between the two and which are opposed to any disparaging conceptions of Horatio. In other words, Horatio cannot be strong and full of self-command, and at the same time have no mind of his own and be easily led around by the nose. I will go more fully into Horatio's character presently, but I think I can say now without fear of contradiction that if for the sake of argument we disregard his friendship for Hamlet, we have no other reason for believing him in any sense weak. Furthermore, as I traced in a previous chapter the state of Hamlet's mind just before he utters these words of praise, I think I made clear the weakness with which the Prince is approaching a tense climax. His sense of Horatio's compensating strength is not likely to be imaginary, much less a subconscious gratitude for the other's companionship.

But, however we defend Hamlet's opinion of his friend we are left with the fact that the Prince is praising Horatio's strength and stoical autonomy; these are admirable qualities, but not enough to make Horatio an interesting dramatic portrayal, nor even likely to attract an idealist who would rather dwell in the realms of angels. Horatio must be seen as a character all by himself, and he must be further seen in the light of whatever it is that attracts him to Hamlet.

Horatio first appears before us in the very opening scene of the play, the scene in which the ghost appears twice to him and to Bernardo and Marcellus. His most apparent function in this scene is to prove the ghost actual and not imaginary; not only is he one more witness to the ghost, but his reluctance to believe the others have seen anything more than the tricks of their own imaginations makes him a reliable witness, one who has to be convinced before he will accept. However, the importance of this dramatic function as well as the importance of the scene itself in setting the atmosphere for the play that is to follow, may tend to obscure certain revelations about Horatio's character. It begins to unfold here in a number of important ways which fit perfectly his later friendship with Hamlet and even help to explain it. The scene begins with the changing of the guard upon the rampart of the castle at midnight. Time and place are thereby established, and from the conversation that follows it is evident that Marcellus has told Horatio of an apparition that has twice appeared during the course of the night watch. The first fact to be noted is Horatio's disbelief in the apparition and his certainty that it will not appear:

> MAR. Horatio says 'tis but our fantasy,
> And will not let belief take hold of him
> Touching this dreaded sight twice seen of us.
> Therefore I have entreated him along
> With us to watch the minutes of this night,
> That if again this apparition come,
> He may approve our eyes and speak of it.
> HOR. Tush, tush, 'twill not appear.

But while Horatio disbelieves the other two he betrays no tendency to laugh or ridicule them for insisting they have seen it. Nor is there any indication that Bernardo and Marcellus resent his disbelieving their story, even though Bernardo says pointedly

> . . . let us once again assail your ears,
> That are so fortified against our story,
> What we have two nights seen.

It is not the cynic nor the militant skeptic that comes before us here in the person of Horatio. True, he does not believe what the other two are telling him; but he has only their word that a bizarre and extraordinary phenomenon has taken place. They may only have thought they saw it or there may be some natural explanation. Nevertheless he sits down and listens politely, however incredulously, to their story. But the account is suddenly broken off by the appearance of the ghost itself:

MAR. Peace, break thee off. Look where it comes again!
BER. In the same figure, like the King that's dead.
MAR. Thou art a scholar. Speak to it, Horatio.
BER. Looks it not like the King? Mark it, Horatio.
HOR. Most like. It harrows me with fear and wonder.
BER. It would be spoke to.
MAR.   Question it, Horatio.
HOR. What art thou that usurp'st this time of night,
      Together with that fair and warlike form
      In which the majesty of buried Denmark
      Did sometimes march? By Heaven I charge thee,
         speak!
MAR. It is offended.
BER.   See, it stalks away!
HOR. Stay! Speak, speak! I charge thee, speak!
                       (*Exit* GHOST)
MAR. 'Tis gone, and will not answer.
BER. How now, Horatio! You tremble and look pale.
      Is not this something more than fantasy?
      What think you on 't?
HOR. Before my God, I might not this believe
      Without the sensible and true avouch
      Of mine own eyes.

This change in Horatio from disbelief to undeniable conviction is more than a mere device to persuade the audience as to the ghost's reality. There is enough proof elsewhere—Bernardo and Marcellus have seen it, and the ghost reveals things to Hamlet which Hamlet could not have otherwise known—to make Horatio's appearance in this scene (as a mere device) unnecessary. Granted that it strengthens our acceptance of the ghost, it is not for that purpose alone that this much of the scene is incorporated. For in it we see a kind of conversion in Horatio that bears a strong connection to his subsequent friendship with Hamlet. It is not a conversion in the sense of acquiring a new faith, or that Horatio is changed in any special way, but that he is brought face to face with something to which heretofore he had been inclined to be indifferent. How indifferent? It is difficult to say whether

Horatio had ever thought much about ghosts prior to this instance; it is practically certain he has never seen one before. But are we to assume he absolutely disbelieves in the reality of visitations *per se* irrespective of his refusal to believe that Bernardo and Marcellus have witnessed the appearance of one? Later in the same scene he speaks of the ghosts which "did squeak and gibber in the Roman streets" when great Julius Caesar fell, indicating a serious consideration of them which is unlikely to be the result of his having seen one on this occasion himself. Between the extremes of thorough belief and thorough disbelief there is broad territory. Many who would accept the possibility of ghosts, or any other supernatural phenomena, are not prepared to accept as true every story they hear about them. Nor is the uncanny any less frightening when we are brought face to face with it simply because we have always taken it for granted. To believe in miracles is no guarantee of remaining unimpressed when we see one performed. As in the case of Hamlet himself, it is the unusual experience becoming real and meaningful (because personal), rather than an absolutely new reality filling a hitherto vacant part of existence. The meaningfulness, the significance is new, not the phenomenon itself. Were Horatio an absolute disbeliever in what he is about to witness, he would have refused to come to the rampart; or coming, he would not have listened patiently to a repetition of what Bernardo and Marcellus insist they have seen.

The effect of the ghost's appearance is immediate. Horatio's brief utterance,

> Before my God, I might not this believe
> Without the sensible and true avouch
> Of mine own eyes.

is the invincible reaction of the man both compelled and willing to accept what he sees before his very eyes. It is dynamic. He trembles and looks pale. But he soon recovers his self-possession, without fetching for a comforting disbelief of his own senses, without any tendency toward hilarity or disrepect or worldly cynicism; there is none of the reaction such as we have already seen in Hamlet following a period of trial or tension. Horatio's temperament does not bound unguided in sportive gyrations the moment it experiences release; on the contrary, he is quite serious and very much concerned as to the meaning of what he has just witnessed. Horatio here betrays not the slightest impulse, voluntary or involuntary, to escape anything. He does not refuse to face facts or cast any soothing lights over what appears to be so ominous. Nor is his self-command the result of any conscious effort on his part to take possession of himself or to allay whatever fears have seized him. His behavior, so balanced where Hamlet's is so mercurial, is like Hamlet's in this: it is entirely unfeigned. Horatio is naturally the way he is. And in the most natural way in the world he speculates upon what "eruption to our state" this visitation bodes, and tells at some length of the recent history of events between Norway and Denmark which explains the present preparations for war. That the ghost may have some connection with all this, that in any event it portends something dire, Horatio is sure of:

> A mote it is to trouble the mind's eye.
> In the most high and palmy state of Rome,
> A little ere the mightiest Julius fell,
> The graves stood tenantless, and the sheeted dead
> Did squeak and gibber in the Roman streets.
> As stars with trains of fire and dews of blood,
> Disasters in the sun, and the moist star
> Upon whose influence Neptune's empire stands
> Was sick almost to doomsday with eclipse.
> And even the like precurse of fierce events,
> As harbingers preceding still the fates
> And prologue to the omen coming on,
> Have Heaven and earth together demonstrated
> Unto our climatures and countrymen.

The tenor of this speech is practical, not psychical, not mystical. The subject is a strange one, but so is the experience that has inspired it. Undoubtedly some mystical re-action is at work within the mind of Horatio—a visit with a ghost could hardly be expected to produce less—but outwardly his considerations are all of a practical nature. Some change has been wrought in him but it is simply that of accepting a supernatural marvel, the real significance of which is its connection with the world all about him. The supernatural, the more than material, does not occupy his speculations. His concern is what such manifestations may mean concerning future events.

But it is quite apparent that this change, small and insignificant though it may appear to be, is complete within itself. Special pains seem to have been taken by the author to make this fact clear. When the ghost appeared the first time Horatio trembled and looked pale. But this can hardly have been due to any sense of personal danger, for when the ghost re-enters upon the rampart Horatio faces up to it regardless of consequences to himself.

> Lo where it comes again!
> I'll cross it, though it blast me.

It must be granted that when Horatio trembled and looked pale at his first sight of the apparition, such signs betokened a tremendous reaction within him. But it is necessary for the dramatist to let us know that this was not on account of base or servile fear. For what other purpose could Shakespeare have had the ghost appear twice in this scene? When Horatio first saw the ghost his state of conviction was staggered, his incredulity swept away as he tremblingly saw what he had refused to accept. This second time there is no such refusal. Acceptance is there and Horatio faces what he now knows to be real:

> Stay, illusion!
> If thou hast any sound, or use of voice,
> Speak to me.
> If there be any good thing to be done
> That may to thee do ease and grace to me,
> Speak to me.

If thou art privy to thy country's fate,
Which, happily, foreknowing may avoid,
Oh, speak!
Or if thou hast uphoarded in thy life
Extorted treasure in the womb of earth,
For which, they say, you spirits oft walk in death,
Speak of it. Stay, and speak!

The courage manifested in this speech clarifies any misconception we may have as to his trembling pallor in the first instance, without reducing it in any way or making it any less powerful. In the absence of any attempt on Horatio's part to instill courage into himself, and in view of the very evident courage he does show when the ghost reappears, it is logical for us to conclude that the passage from a kind of disbelief to firm belief is no phlegmatic or composed one. It is emotional, because it is deep. Those who see Horatio as unimaginative overlook the meaning of all these details which comprise the dramatist's first introduction of this character, a thing always to be carefully noted in Shakespeare.

Now, many may insist that all this only goes back to proving the reality of the ghost; that everything I say is true enough, but that Horatio's "conversion" and all of them noting the ghost's resemblance to the dead king— these are nothing more than powerful arguments at the very opening of the play that the spectre which later imparts the details of a murder to Hamlet is something more than imaginary. The answer to this is that in no other play has Shakespeare gone to such lengths to prove a ghost's reality. From the internal evidence of other plays the difference between a live ghost and a disordered fancy is clearly but very briefly indicated. The people of Shakespeare's time believed in ghosts and it was unnecessary to pile up evidence and corroborating witnesses of varying degrees of skepticism. This helps, of course, because of the unusual and even improbable nature of the thing seen. But we must remember that if we reduce this particular part of the play to one of ghost-proving and mood-setting, we cannot escape the fact that both rely heavily on the character of Horatio. What I have said about him in no way lessens the usefulness of this opening scene in these two points; it strengthens it. Nevertheless it is a strengthening that becomes somewhat superfluous when we bear in mind all of the additional proof contained in the play. Hamlet's long conversation with the ghost in Act I, Sc. v, would of itself dispel any doubts, and while Hamlet later has misgivings as to trusting the ghost this is not because he has any doubts as to its actual existence but because he thinks it may have been an evil spirit:

> The spirit that I have seen
> May be the Devil, and the Devil hath power
> To assume a pleasing shape. Yea, and perhaps
> Out of my weakness and my melancholy,
> As he is very potent with such spirits,
> Abuses me to damn me.

Consequently, we may safely conclude that the introductory scene serves purposes other than to belabor a point about which there should be no reasonable difficulty.

Whatever we may deduce from these revelations, whether much or little, it is immediately clear that Horatio fits no classification conventionally assigned to those who say but little. He is not what is called "the strong, silent type," if by that we mean emotionless and intellectually slow. He is not boorish. He is not morose like Don John. He is not disgruntled, insouciant, unconcerned, listless. Select an adjective which you think describes the strong silent type and see if it can be fairly said to describe Horatio as we see him in the first two scenes of the play. He is *not* especially silent. The notion of Horatio's laconism comes, if it comes at all, from scenes much later on. When we first meet him he speaks quite freely and easily, betraying not the slightest inclination to silence, and is consequently innocent of anything, good or bad, which might be attributed to the silent type. It may be said that these later scenes outnumber the earlier ones, and we might better infer Horatio's character by seeing how he behaves most of the time rather than by a few minority instances—a kind of averaging-out process in which his periods of brevity of speech far outweigh those of his loquacity. This is a question to be postponed for the moment, for it represents a change with much significance attached to it. It *is* a change, however. It is not quite the same Horatio we see here in the beginning, and many ideas concerning him overlook completely his initial appearance. As I have said, initial appearances are important in Shakespeare. The dramatist realizes the audience is glimpsing a character for the first time, and while a particular character may appear different in later scenes the change is perfectly consistent with the action of the play. No one in his first appearance is ever "out of character," in the sense that he behaves in such a way as to mislead the audience. Shakespeare cannot incorporate a long and deep portrayal of individual traits at this point; he must be economical and clear. But the mere fact that the details are brief does not render them immaterial. Horatio is exhibited under the pressure of a highly emotional experience and not in an ordinary passage of calm dialogue devoid of purpose and barren of character implications.

We learn that Horatio does not believe too readily a story of the supernatural, though he is not jeeringly cynical in his attitude; that, once convinced, he is as convinced as anyone and even looks for meaning in what he has previously doubted; that he is courageous; that he is affable and conversational. We learn also that he is a scholar, a fact reasonable enough for us to accept in view of his having been a student at Wittenberg. He seems well up on current events and national affairs. In all he says and does he gives every indication of being an intelligent young man. This picture of Horatio is clear enough without being particularly deep or even interesting; many a minor character has been portrayed with equal clarity. We must bear in mind, nevertheless, that it does not square with disparaging concepts formed from his markedly different manner in later scenes. If he is different then from what he is now it is because a profound change comes over him, and just what that change is and the reasons for it are what we have to seek.

The next time we see Horatio is in the following scene when he comes with Bernardo and Marcellus to tell Hamlet about the ghost. It is evident from the way Hamlet greets Horatio that the two men cannot have been very close friends in the past. Hamlet's "Horatio—or I do forget myself" indicates that the Prince remembers him but is not quite certain of the name. He knows Horatio is a student at Wittenberg, having undoubtedly seen him there many times and talked with him, and he knows him well enough to deny the "truant disposition" of which Horatio accuses himself. All this would suggest acquaintanceship, perhaps something bordering on friendship, but certainly not a warm friendship of long standing. Their being together at Wittenberg cannot have been very long ago, and in all probability is less than the two months since the elder Hamlet's death; Hamlet's momentary doubt as to Horatio's identity is not the result of any prolonged separation from him, nor is it the result of any emotional upset on the part of the Prince. By Hamlet's words, "Horatio—or I do forget myself," he names the other first, and then suggests he may be mistaken. He betrays no evidence of perplexity prior to naming him or that he recognizes a face but cannot place the name. Nor is Hamlet's emotional upset the kind that is likely to render him incapable of remembering people whom he very well knows. He is sad, heartbroken, disillusioned; he is not afflicted with a narcosis of inattention.

Taking the evidence as we find it, then, we may say that the friendship between Horatio and Hamlet (the friendship as we know it in the play) begins *during* and *not before* the play. They never recall old times they have had together, or refer to anything that would suggest a friendship that goes back over the years. Horatio has been at Elsinore since the elder Hamlet's funeral, yet he and

149

Hamlet have not seen each other and Hamlet does not know his fellow student is away from Wittenberg until this moment. Those who would insist that this is the resumption and not the beginning of a close friendship, might point to the warm sentiments expressed by Hamlet right after the exchange of greetings:

HAML. But what, in faith, make you from Wittenberg?
HOR. A truant disposition, good my lord.
HAML. I would not hear your enemy say so,
Nor shall you do my ear that violence
To make it truster of your own report
Against yourself. I know you are no truant.
But what is your affair in Elsinore?
We'll teach you to drink deep ere you depart.

Certainly Hamlet does not say this to a mere acquaintance.

It does seem a warm sentiment to express to someone whose name he was not certain of a few seconds ago, but this cannot dismiss the evidence already presented; in addition to which there is a deeper and far more subconscious explanation. The earlier part of this scene presents with increasing emphasis the aloneness of Hamlet in his world. The tearful soliloquy which climaxes this aloneness builds towards its own climax when Hamlet says

But break, my heart, for I must hold my tongue!

This is the point toward which the scene has been leading, for it expresses the epitome of his sorrow and of the absence of anyone to share it with him. As he chokingly speaks these words, he falls into a chair and sobs quietly for several moments. The scene has been dramatically arranged so as to clarify any misconceptions and to work, through a series of audience reactions, toward that moment when we are psychologically at one with Hamlet and sharing to the full his rejection of what we momentarily accepted earlier. As he sits weeping in the center of the now deserted stage, he becomes the silent embodiment of his own estrangement and grief. Words have said all that can be said. The brief tableau must convey to us the final measure of Hamlet's heartbreak. The room we look upon recalls in that uncanny fashion the array of courtly personages that filled every corner of it and whose footsteps have scarcely died away and left it to the one remaining figure and his brooding solitude. Hamlet, clad in black, creates quite another atmosphere, the more striking because we still remember the others and associate them with it. It is at this point that Horatio appears, the same Horatio whose qualities we have had a chance to learn in the scene before. The contrast in Hamlet's mood is too striking to admit of obvious or insignificant explanations, such as the unexpected reappearance of an old friend. Nor is it likely Shakespeare would bring these two men together at this precise psychological moment for no other reason than the fact that Horatio has to tell about the ghost and this is as good a time as any to do it.

The appearance of Horatio and the reaction of Hamlet are both a complete change from the previous part of this scene. Although we know nothing yet of the murder and can glean but little of the characters of those who crowd about the King and then depart, we can sense intuitively some difference between them and Horatio. He is conspicuously absent from this gathering of people who are interested in being so lighthearted though they must profane the dead to do so. Their most serious considerations are trivialities compared with Hamlet's suffering or Horatio's encounter with the spirit of the deceased King. A wholesome change is immediately forced upon the reader by the very juxtaposition of the two parts of the one scene. The change is most directly brought out by the sympathy of feeling between the Prince and Horatio:

HOR.	My lord, I came to see your father's funeral.
HAML.	I pray thee do not mock me, fellow student.
	I think it was to seem my mother's wedding.
HOR.	Indeed, my lord, it followed hard upon.
HAML.	Thrift, thrift, Horatio! The funeral baked meats
	Did coldly furnish forth the marriage tables.
	Would I had met my dearest foe in Heaven
	Or ever I had seen that day, Horatio!

My father!—Methinks I see my father.

HOR.   Oh, where, my lord?

HAML.   In my mind's eye, Horatio.

HOR.   I saw him once. He was a goodly King.

HAML.   He was a man, take him for all in all.
              I shall not look upon his like again.

Horatio's admission that the Queen's remarriage follow-ed "hard upon" the funeral of her first husband, and his conviction that the dead King was a "goodly King" are pointed expressions of such sympathy. But they are fol-low-ups. They are a proof of sympathy that is already indicated before Horatio actually expresses it. Hamlet warms to Horatio *before* Horatio renders anything like condolence for what must be tormenting the Prince. It is, therefore, a kind of kinship which is sensed—and *immedi-ately* sensed—rather than one based on sentiments that pass between them. In the final analysis all deep friendship must transcend manifestations and reasons that may be factually observed. This is not to deny the importance of the obvious. Friendships have sprung from things that can definitely be pinpointed, and they have deepened in the same way. But no matter how completely we catalogue the more observable causes of true friendship, we are still left with the conclusion that there is "something else." On the other hand much can be known about this some-thing else, or what constitutes the more important, the essential part of friendship; it cannot be known complete-ly, but neither is it unknowable. The point to be stressed is that it is a different thing entirely from the outward phenomena that may be supposed to be responsible for its birth and growth. Now, the dramatist faces a difficulty in portraying the commencement of an affinity that comes to be as deep as that between Horatio and Hamlet; if it is shown to stem from palpable causes (such as Horatio's ex-pressions of sympathy) it is in danger of being attributed only to those causes, and consequently lessened in the eye of the audience. There would be some justification in say-ing that Hamlet turns to Horatio because Horatio is the only one who is sympathetic to him in his double bereavement. Hamlet's feeling here would be, in some sense, gratitude rather than communion. I do not deny that such sympathy is an important thing in itself—I have spoken elsewhere of the effect on Hamlet where it is lacking. But the fact remains that although Hamlet has just groaned upon the world as an unweeded garden possessed by things rank and gross in nature, he speaks now with surprising warmth to Horatio and speaks prior to the utterance of anything that would inspire such warmth. And, in view of everything I have cited before, this is the first time he has ever felt close to Horatio. In the soliloquy just prior to Horatio's entry where Hamlet condemns the world, there is no indication that there are any exceptions. It might be said that Horatio may simply have slipped Hamlet's mind; after all, in the "To be or not to be" soliloquy Hamlet draws a not very pretty picture of the world (he fails to admit even the palliative of a sincere friendship) although he and Horatio have certainly become close friends by that time. This is true enough, but that soliloquy bears special reference to the duty under which Hamlet is laboring; it lists the ills of life without sweepingly condemning it as sterile. In the scene we are considering, Hamlet does not yet know of his father's murder, and his violent antipathy is the immediate result of observing all the people around him. What they do hurts him. His failure to include or exclude Horatio is more than momentary forgetfulness since he is not even certain of Horatio's identity.

The important thing about this friendship between Hamlet and Horatio, right from its inception, is that there is something inexpressible and perfectly natural about it. Instinctively something is felt. I have said before that there was a time when Hamlet accepted the world and all the people in it as ideal; this was not a burning belief, a positive faith in humanity; rather it was a state of semi-indifference, a false acceptance of the world rather than a false conviction as to its nature. Actually he did not know or think too much about it, betraying that tendency toward unconcern that comes with general well-being. He was not discriminating. With all going well there was really no reason for discrimination of any kind. No doubt Hamlet thought Horatio as fine as anyone else, but no finer. He was one among many just like him, and though this was an injustice to Horatio, it is the most probable reason why he and Hamlet did not become close friends the sooner. Not only was the ideal friend a commonplace thing, but the ideal friend had far less importance prior to the collapse of Hamlet's world about his ears. When this happens and the world becomes a barren place, Horatio is probably forgotten for the time being along with many another person Hamlet must have known at Wittenberg. But suddenly and unexpectedly Horatio reappears. We do not stretch things too far when we conjecture that Hamlet is not without some innate awareness of Horatio's character for the first time. Such intuitive sensing of another's true self is by no means unusual under the pressure of extreme personal sorrow, and the fact that Hamlet sees now what he overlooked before convinces him far more than if he were meeting Horatio for the first time and seeing him correctly.

It is fairly simple to decide in what way Hamlet is attracted to Horatio, but it is not so simple to decide why or how Horatio is attracted to Hamlet. The Prince states his own feelings very succinctly in the lines I have previously quoted, and they constitute a very true summation of Horatio's character. Hamlet's opinion bears out what we have observed with respect to the opening scene. It is easy to understand why a changeable and vacillating person like Hamlet would be drawn to the more constant and self-controlled Horatio. But Horatio never says a word about why he feels so close to Hamlet. Nor is it immediately apparent what quality in Hamlet would appeal to Horatio—Hamlet who has attracted yet puzzled so many millions of people. This is what I wish to deal with in the rest of this chapter. And I wish once and for all to dispense with the notion of Horatio being a mere follower or hanger-on of Hamlet as entirely inconsistent with any real study of the man. Since the friendship is a maturing and harmonious communion of two souls, it is unlikely that they would ever have serious disagreements about anything. But it is worthy of note that there are times in the second ghost scene when Horatio does not see eye to eye with Hamlet. These are indeed trifles, but they are trifles in the sense that they are tiny bits of revelation like little marks and curves in the sketch of a person's face. First there is Horatio's persistence in forbidding Hamlet to follow the ghost, even though Hamlet finally overrules him. When Hamlet, after having talked with the ghost, makes the inexplicable comment, "There's ne'er a villain dwelling in all Denmark but he's an arrant knave," Horatio's retort is common sense itself: "There needs no ghost, my lord, come from the grave to tell us this." And again, "These are but wild and whirling words, my lord." Unimportant as these things may appear to be, they help constitute a character that has an individuality of its own, one not likely to become passive under the spell of another. There is nothing of the sycophant or the jackal about him.

Thus, we have a chance to study Horatio whose character is consistent through three separate scenes. In his maturing friendship with Hamlet he says little, he who has betrayed no natural disinclination to speech at the beginning of the play; he becomes almost passive although he has been introduced to us as anything but the passive type. And this change does not come immediately but gradually, after the passage of months during which time he has the opportunity of coming to know Hamlet more and more deeply. His knowledge of the Prince and his feeling for him are of simultaneous development; each grows as the other does. Yet the more we examine just what it is that Horatio knows about Hamlet, the further we are from any conspicuously clear explanations as to the love that comes as a result of it. Horatio is the only one in the play who knows of the Prince's failure to avenge the death of his royal father. How much he could divine from Hamlet's first meeting with the ghost or precisely when Hamlet told him of Claudius's guilt, we cannot definitely say; but we know from their conversation just prior to the play that Hamlet has informed his friend of the circumstances of his father's death, the reason for the play, and the fact that the ghost revealed the dreadful secret. Horatio knows the time that has passed without anything being accomplished. He witnesses the King's guilty behavior during the performance of the play, the proof which Hamlet says he needs, yet which fails to precipitate the Prince into any consequent action. Furthermore, Horatio can very easily reason out additional motives for Hamlet to take steps. He is certainly aware of the compoundings of Claudius's crime, such as the present position of Gertrude and the fact that the King is a usurper.

From the sentiments Horatio utters to Hamlet at the beginning he is not personally indifferent to what Hamlet must feel; and if he ever had any doubts as to the character of Claudius (exclusive of what he already knows) such doubts are resolved in Act V, Sc. ii, when Hamlet tells of the King's plan to have him put to death in England. Horatio's amazed exclamation, "Why, what a King is this!" carries a bookful of condemnation. Certainly he is aware of every motive, large or small, practical or honorable, which Prince Hamlet has for bringing justice to bear on King Claudius. Yet Horatio never says a word, even to himself, about Hamlet's procrastination, nor does he give the slightest indication he thinks any less of him for his inexplicable delays. On the contrary, Horatio's love grows stronger and stronger. Admittedly this love is inferred from their constant companionship and by Horatio's occasionally addressing Hamlet as "sweet lord" or some other such expression, which, it may be argued, are terms of courtesy rather than terms of endearment. No evidence could be more positive, however, than Horatio's desire to follow Hamlet in death. "I am more an antique Roman than a Dane," says Horatio as Hamlet lies mortally wounded. He actually reaches for the poisoned cup and is prevented only when Hamlet struggles to take it from him and begs Horatio to live after him and tell his story. Horatio must face the harsh world now without his beloved friend, absent himself from felicity awhile and draw the breath of pain. After Hamlet dies Horatio gives vent to that brief speech, the emotion and sincerity of which cannot be denied:

> Now cracks a noble heart. Good night, sweet Prince,
> And flights of angels sing thee to thy rest!

Eloquence itself could not say more. While Horatio is not naturally uncommunicative, neither is he given to emotionalizing unless he be profoundly stirred. He is a man who says what he means without ever overstating his feelings or pretending what he does not feel. Nor is there the slightest reason for thinking his sorrowing farewell to the departed Hamlet results from Hamlet's having at long last killed his father's murderer or that it is in any way a warming up to the Prince after a period of cooling. It is not the result of Hamlet's having at last vindicated his honor. Horatio's love grows unabated throughout the play and his "Now cracks a *noble heart*!" is but the saying of what has long been unsaid. It is the climactic expression of a sincere and profoundly beautiful friendship which the Elizabethan always spoke of as love and which is so different from the mild-mannered intercourse of agreeable companionship.

When we see all this in its true light we can dismiss any such notion as the one that Horatio's devotion to Hamlet is one of loyalty. Horatio of course realizes Hamlet is the rightful Prince and the King a usurper; his loyalty would naturally be to the young Prince and not to the lawless Claudius. Loyalty he undoubtedly has since he is the only other person who knows Claudius murdered the former King, and this would hold weight with Horatio regardless of any personal affinity he might have with the rightful heir to the throne. But to say that this entirely explains the Hamlet-Horatio association is to ignore too many things in the play. A mere sense of justice would not induce the even-tempered Horatio to wish to follow Hamlet in death. If he wanted to give his life in the service of his Prince, or to save him, loyalty alone might be said to be his motive; but Hamlet has already received a mortal wound and the villainous King now lies dead. Horatio's desire to drink the remaining poison cannot possibly be explained as an attempt to serve the state or his rightful leader, nor does he ever speak or behave as one actuated only by loyalty. Long after he and Hamlet have proof of the King's guilt, Horatio moves about the court obeying orders, apparently with perfect resignation. That he is not a hypocrite or a time-server, we know. He who has taken fortune's buffets and rewards with equal thanks, is also a stoic in that he lives with poise and equanimity in places where corruption, which is not his to correct, leaves him uncontaminated. That Hamlet is better than all this impresses Horatio. But his reaction to Hamlet cannot be seen as a cold and analytical thing of simple legality; rather Horatio's continual companionship must be thought to proceed from a much warmer sense of something further by which he sees the person and human failings as well as the virtues of Hamlet.

What, I ask, attracts Horatio to Hamlet? Certainly, while he may not be aware of Hamlet's mental turmoil (a moot question at best), he must realize how much time has passed without anything having been done to right a terrible wrong. If, unthinkable as it is, this never entered his mind, he might be expected to show some surprise, and perhaps disapproval, when Hamlet sums up his position after having told Horatio of the King's attempt on his, Hamlet's, life:

> Does it not, think'st thee, stand me now upon—
> He that hath killed my King and whored my mother,
> Popped in between the election and my hopes,

Thrown out his angle for my proper life,
And with such cozenage—is 't not perfect conscience,
To quit him with this arm? And is 't not to be damned,
To let this canker of our nature come
In further evil?

Horatio betrays not the slightest wonder at Hamlet upon hearing this, and the reason he does not is that he has known it perfectly well all along. And yet this man, the one character in the play who knows Hamlet as he really is, loves him with a love that is unshakable; the others, who see only the outward excellences and have no suspicions whatever of his failure to carry through a task enjoined upon him, who see nothing of the inner man—these are all opposed to him or indifferent to him in one way or another. By all laws of worldly logic he should be better as they see him than as Horatio does. But it is just the opposite. And all of them who talk so much about Hamlet do not even begin to know him as Horatio knows him—Horatio who says nothing. We look in vain for a reason that will fully explain this. We seek a word from Horatio himself, but he is silent. It is a strange silence and one of the most pregnant things in all Shakespeare. In it lies the key to this mysterious friendship which begins only at a point when Hamlet's other attachments have already been long in existence. It eclipses all the others until they seem more like estrangements than friendships. Duration will not explain it nor is it the result of having shared any great number of the harsh experiences of life together. It seems to consist exclusively of that unfathomable "something else" of which I have spoken previously. Without wishing to conjecture too far upon what appears to be in total darkness, we can at least be certain of the *type* of friendship that exists between this pair, and thereby lean in the direction of what gives rise to it. This is easily done if we keep in mind the basic points of what I have already laid down. Horatio is strong, intelligent, and self-possessed. His friendship with Hamlet begins and matures during the course of the play. He knows of Hamlet's failures. Yet he undergoes a kind of metamorphosis which renders his manner toward the Prince one of love and quiet humility. Only the deepest kind of attraction could occasion such a relationship.

It would be monotonous repetition to go over again the subject of Hamlet's idealism. I have attempted to show that his very imperfections betoken virtuous qualities that reach far beyond the petty concerns of life at the court of Denmark. The pertinent question, however, still remains: does Horatio sense the supposed angelic soul of Hamlet? And if we say yes, what are our reasons for saying so? In the first place the absence of any other reasons (not only the absence, but actual controverting evidence as to their possibility) is a powerful argument in itself. His love for Hamlet is not indiscriminate and without cause. Neither are his words after Hamlet's death. If Horatio sees Hamlet as intimately as we do, if Hamlet's nobility of character can be amply demonstrated, and if Horatio's final opinion coincides pretty closely with our own, we can certainly conclude that Horatio sees what we see. It is not likely he would talk about it to any great extent, because such things are more easily felt than put into words. It is enough for us that what he does say is sufficient.

In addition, it is a consistent characteristic of Shakespeare's balanced characters, i. e., those who walk the level of life, that they know good from bad, the lovable from the hateful, the perfect from the mediocre. Friar Laurence, York, Blunt, Enobarbus, all base their opinions upon some concept of a fixed scale of right and wrong. One notable exception to this is Buckingham in *Richard III*, but since he is so definitely an exception and since he is involved in circumstances so fraught with villainy and suspicion as to admit of no goodness anywhere, we can eliminate him and confine ourselves to his counterparts in happier plays. But with respect to these others we may say of them that they are not simply average people. In fact, it is a great error to think the man who walks the level of life in Shakespeare is nothing but a median or midpoint among the divergencies of the other characters. This would be inevitably so if Shakespeare had believed man to be the measure of all things. For then the constant shift and interplay of other men's behavior would determine a kind of locus along which we might look for the thoroughly average person to be found. But Shakespeare's balanced characters are quite the reverse. Either they do not change at all (regardless of the changes all about them), or, if they do, the change is not simply a realignment of themselves with new sets of norms. They are indeed aware of other people's behavior, but not as patterns or criteria for their own. That is to say, a balanced character may be influenced by others, but social behavior *per se* will not determine what his is to be. We see too many examples in which level-of-life characters are too outspoken and disapproving, sometimes with a somewhat violent condemnation as in the case of Friar Laurence toward Romeo, to be considered neutral driftwood. The whole point of including the balanced character in the first place, is to have a kind of fixed standard of fairly normal conduct against which we can measure the wicked man's wickedness, the good man's virtue, the happy man's joy, and so on. By whatever length these others differ from the balanced man, by so much are their individuating traits emphasized. If such a character were no more than a hypothetical mean among many extremes he would serve little dramatic purpose, because his position would be determined by that of the others, instead of theirs by his.

But it is not only that the level-of-life character acts in a standard way. His views are equally well balanced. He sees all correctly. In addition to Horatio's function of providing a kind of midpoint about which other characters are arranged, there is the fact of his preference for Hamlet. Horatio confirms what we instinctively feel. A balanced view, an undistorted vision, a judgment neither corrupted by hopes of worldly gain nor stunted by ignorance, a cool and calm temper that cannot be accused of rashness—all of these go to make up the character of him who becomes Hamlet's sincere and admiring friend. His eyes are upon Hamlet and he is silent. We need not be so hyperbolical as to say he is filled with awe, but certainly Shakespeare has pointed up this silence of Horatio and intended it to be noted. It is hardly necessary to wait for Horatio's words at Hamlet's death in order to infer what his silence has meant all along. It is profound and meaningful, and it is so strikingly at variance with the manner of similar characters in other plays that we may look for something profound as the occasion for it.

Friar Laurence is forced to attempt the active role of peacemaker amid the hate of two feuding families. He must perform, he must actually connive for the welfare of others. There is no question as to his assertive, though unavailing, course of action. He says much and he does much. He continually projects himself into the lives and affairs of other people, though we never think of him as a particularly interfering kind of person. In all he says and does we are perfectly clear, for the simple reason that his attention is focused upon things that are plainly evident. There is nothing abstruse about the feud between the Capulets and Montagues, or Romeo's uncontrollability, or the consequences of disregarding princely authority. The play is concerned with these things and the Friar speaks of them as with the detachment of a commentator or chorus, yet with the interest of a holy man whose concern is the lives and spiritual welfare of those around him. He clarifies the subject of the play by his own attitude toward it.

A similar, though less active function is that of Blunt in *Henry IV*, Part I. He has not the responsibility of Friar Laurence, but he does have a choice to make. In the civil war between the King's forces and the rebels he must side with one or the other. So must everyone else, but while the others all have personal inclinations that put them in one camp or the other, Blunt is friendly to both and his choice must be based on the righteousness of whichever cause he espouses. The choice is not an obvious one since each side has arguments to support it. Nevertheless a choice must be made and Blunt's decision to support the King comes of an unbiased conviction that, all things considered, he must oppose those who "stand against annointed Majesty." An even more difficult position is that of York in *Richard II*. First, he supports Richard as the rightful king, despite Richard's glaring misdeeds about which he, York, has spoken out as strongly as anyone. Yet, when Richard is deposed and surrenders the crown to Bolingbroke, York becomes the sworn servant of the new king. It is very shallow reading of York's character to see him as a mere time-server in this. He is too stern a moralist, too outspoken in perilous situations; his personal sympathies are ever with Richard even though he will condemn his own son for treason to Henry. In the delicate situation wherein a rebellion, largely justifiable though technically wrong, is successful, York seems to have no choice but what is evil. If he sides with Henry he condones a rebellion against the true monarch. If he sides with Richard he espouses an evil king as well as a hopeless cause. It is true that he does not foresee the future bloodshed that will result from the usurpation, as the Bishop of Carlisle does; nevertheless, he must endorse a government capable of maintaining itself and ending the seething unrest among the people. The deplorable state of affairs is not of his making, but he must assist in finding an immediate solution. Thus, York concentrates our attention on the very heart of the tragedy: its political dilemma, the moral evil on both sides of the issue, personal sympathies and antipathies. Rarely has Shakespeare so skillfully worked a character into every entanglement of the plot, and at the same time preserved a balance of judgment that enables that character to speak with such feeling and such fairness. York is no coldhearted analyst. Seldom does he speak without the emotion of the moment coming to his lips. He is our entry into the events that lead up to the tragedy of Richard. Know York, feel with him, and you see and feel the pulsing life of those times without ever losing perspective or becoming swayed too strongly in any one direction.

Each of these characters accomplishes this, to a greater or lesser degree. They play an all-exploring beam upon what is vital to the dramas in which they appear. Without them we should certainly have to probe harder into great masses of indefiniteness, with the possibility of no decisive answer to be found. Whether one can be found or no there is little doubt as to the corraborative value of one who sees clearly. The dramatic interest belongs to Richard, to Romeo and Juliet, to King Henry and his son, and Falstaff. The fabric of that interest is illuminated by the perceptive powers of another, and this is what Horatio has in common with these other level-of-life characters. He is in the play for the same reason they are: to help direct our attention and sympathies in the proper direction. Horatio is not an amoralist. He does not regard man's various qualities with an indifferent eye; he does not see them as mere components of a whole, each one as good as the other so long as all are in their proper amount. He is acutely aware of right and wrong, as most of the unbalanced characters in the play are not, and he recognizes what should be avoided and what pursued. He senses intuitively that, however perfectly balanced a man may be, he is not ideal because of that. The ideal man, or the man closer to the ideal, is likely to be a misfit in life; and it is the curious truth that the man of balance will sooner recognize all misfits for what they are, angels or devils. He will incline toward one and avoid the other. Perfectly harmonious men, socially desirable though they may be, can never be the ideal or aim of all men, since man will still desire something higher. And none realizes this so completely as the perfectly balanced man himself.

The position Horatio occupies is not one in which he would be called upon to deliver opinions. He has not the religious responsibility to preach as Friar Laurence has, nor the political obligation to speak out in time of national crisis as York has; he is not a go-between to parley with the opposition as Blunt is. Notwithstanding this, however, it is unthinkable that Horatio would speak about what he focuses our attention upon, even to himself in the form of a soliloquy. The subject of an individual's beauty of soul is a deep and profound one, a mystical one. It is sensed. It is not put into words as are the more apparent things of which York and Friar Laurence have so much to say. As unmistakably as it may be comprehended, it becomes an enigma when we would say just what we have seen; in point of fact, it is seldom if ever that we are called upon to explain such things and we are perfectly content to remain silent about them. Certainly no one in the play would dream of questioning Horatio as to what he perceives in the noble Prince, particularly since everyone else has remained so blindly indifferent to Hamlet; or if anyone were to become mildly interested, Horatio would have sufficient worldy wisdom to "answer the fool according to his folly," and ward off the interlocutor with something within his ken. With the audience it is different. We know that Horatio is being silent *about* something, and a careful reading of everything pertinent to his character from the very first scene down to his final words at the close, demonstrates that his silence can mean only one thing. Once Shakespeare has made that clear, this silence does not render Horatio's reaction to Hamlet less intelligible, but more profound.

As Hamlet represents the true nature of man in this world, so Horatio represents the view we should take of him—if our minds and hearts be right. Taken together the two men make the play the grand and universal thing it is; their relationship removes the drama once and for all from the realms of the obvious and the lesser. It becomes something immeasurably greater than a simple tragedy about a man who has to kill a king and does not get an opportunity to do it, or cannot make up his mind how to do it, or shrinks from regicide; or about a man secretly in revolt against false notions of honor and revenge, or who has an Oedipus complex, or any of the other convenient formulas that justify a full-length play of meaningless delays and unrelated incidents of swordplay and ghosts and commentaries on the emptiness of life. All these things are only parts of the tragedy of *Hamlet*. To see them in combination is to descry something infinitely more, something which can never be directly expressed. Some things we can know. But, to quote Hamlet just before he dies,

The rest is silence.

VI

GRAVEYARD SCENE

The graveyard scene may be divided into two parts; the first concerns the gravediggers and the philosophizing of Hamlet upon the subject of death, the second the burial of Ophelia. The most evident purpose of the entire scene is to provide an ironic contrast between the gravediggers' unfeeling humor plus Hamlet's grim irony on one side, and the startling revelation on the other that it is Ophelia for whom the grave is being prepared. However, even this may be missed to a large extent if we regard the gravediggers' jokes as somewhat cruel or in rather poor taste but nothing more; or that Hamlet's examining the skulls represents a kind of morbid fascination, an exaggerated view of death's horror which heightens the effect of Ophelia's funeral procession when it appears. If this were the logical attitude, then the only real reason for the scene's inclusion in the first place would be to show us the burial of Ophelia (the audience already knows of her death) and its effect on Hamlet; but its effect on Hamlet depends greatly upon the first part of the scene. That is to say, Hamlet's behavior at the grave of Ophelia might have been very different had he learned of her death in some other way and in other circumstances. In addition to which, not only does the first part heighten the effect of the second part, but the second part heightens the effect of the first.

The opening portion of this scene is by far the longer of the two, extending through 240 lines. The second part is only 82 lines, or approximately one-third the length of the opening. This first part could be taken by itself as a wonderfully effective scene, even without the funeral of Ophelia, and one which conveys to us a side to Hamlet's character which we do not see revealed elsewhere. It is an Inferno-like wandering through the realms of death, full of grim humor and horror. Skulls are tossed up out of the earth, skulls of those who were known and of those whose identity can only be guessed at; these skulls draw Hamlet to converse with them as if life were still in them. Dead indeed they are, but how much more vivid and gruesome than imaginary shades of the departed! This is climaxed, one might almost say fulfilled, with the tragic discovery that Hamlet's beloved Ophelia is even now to be committed to these gloomy confines.

However, the mood of this scene is very slowly and carefully fashioned, gradually intensified until that climactic moment. It begins in a far different, though not unaccountable, spirit, as we find the gravediggers joking and laughing while they dig a grave for someone who is just another person as far as they are concerned. In addition, all this is not permitted to be misinterpreted, even for a second, as a mere comic interlude. From the very opening lines it is clear whom they are talking about. The previous scene closed with the Queen announcing the drowning of Ophelia, and the first lines of this scene, while they do not name Ophelia, refer to "her" and speak of the "drowning." The contrast between Ophelia's tragic death and the laughing jokes and songs of the two rustics who dig her grave strikes the reader immediately and forcefully. The humor is not toned down nor the jokes any the less designed to provoke laughter, out of any respect for the fact that Ophelia is the one concerned. Humor and tragedy, two irreconcilable opposites, cannot continue to hold the stage together; the tragedy is too tragic and the humor too comical to admit of the tiniest conceivable bit of congruence between the two. The minds of the audience would be compelled either to turn to one and shut the other away, or fall into a kind of synthetic indifference between them. When Hamlet and Horatio enter the yard and hear the gravedigger singing as he digs and throws up skulls, Hamlet cannot help pausing to wonder, "Has this fellow no feeling of his business, that he sings at grave-making?" This thought in Hamlet's mind not only introduces what is to follow, but very simply and pointedly brings out the two extremes on death most generally found in the world (and I stress *death*, rather than the life after death) : utter indifference and ghastly intentness. I do not use the term "ghastly intentness" in any disapproving sense. I use it, and would wish the reader to understand the strict meaning of the words rather than any connotative association they may have with abnormal sensitivity, because it is what we next see in Hamlet as he stoops down to examine the skulls that have been tossed up. Perhaps some readers feel Hamlet thinks too curiously and closely upon the subject of death. He becomes depressing about it, we may be tempted to think, and such thoughts are harrowing.

> That skull had a tongue in it, and could sing once. How the
> knave jowls it to the ground, as if it were Cain's jawbone,

that did the first murder! It might be the pate of a politician which this ass now o'erreaches—one that would circumvent God, might it not?

Or of a courtier, which could say "Good morrow, sweet lord! How dost thou, good lord?" This might be my lord Such-a-one that praised my lord Such-a-one's horse when he meant to beg it, might it not?

These are cheerless thoughts. When Hamlet wonders to what base uses the bones of even the greatest of us may eventually be put, we may possibly agree with Horatio who replies, "T'were to consider too curiously to consider so." Why dwell upon such things at all?

Much as the reader disagrees with the rustics' jokes about death, he perhaps feels that Hamlet wanders too far in the other extreme and instead of a respectful but tempered attitude the Prince plunges into a disconcerting orgy of the horrific. Thus there is a tendency to agree with Horatio who says of the singing gravedigger, "Custom hath made it in him a property of easiness." The gravedigger has seen so much of death that he has stopped thinking of its significance and now regards it merely as part of the day's work. For our part, while we may disapprove of a too eager examination of its ghoulish horrors, we cannot feel it to be so devoid of significance as to be laughed and joked about. Horatio, as the perfectly blended man of the world, speaks the world's view of this; but it is important to note that there is more disapproval in what he says to Hamlet than in what he says of the gravedigger. "T'were to consider too curiously to consider so," though a minor disagreement, is a disagreement nonetheless. He is admonishing the Prince, mildly though he does it, about pursuing such thoughts too far. But Horatio's other remark, "Custom hath made it in him a property of easiness," is an observation, not a judgment. Custom, not the person, is responsible. And custom is regarded with neither approval nor disapproval, but with acceptance. If we, like Horatio, disapprove of Hamlet's "considering too curiously," we too are slightly more

in the direction of the gravedigger's attitude than square-
ly in the middle of the two extremes. Indifference, even
where it is only a limited indifference or an avoidance of
an extreme, tends to be more congenial to total indifference than to total concern. And Horatio, who is singularly aware of the loftiness and sweetness in Hamlet's
nature, cannot forbear wincing when that same nature
discourses on the dreaded eventuality of our material
bodies. Hamlet's reply to Horatio must not be taken as an
arbitrary insistence upon the technical truth of some
casuistry, but rather the plain, honest facts. Disagreeing
that he is pondering too precisely on all this, Hamlet says:

> No, faith, not a jot, but to follow him thither with modesty
> enough and likelihood to lead it. As thus: Alexander died,
> Alexander was buried, Alexander returneth into dust; the
> dust is earth; of earth we make loam; and why of that loam,
> whereto he was converted, might they not stop a beer barrel?

The superfine details with which Hamlet elaborates upon
these things are, in his own words, not exaggerations nor
any undue striving after the horrible, but clear, simple
facts which we ought to be aware of. They serve to make
death so real that it is the reality we shrink from. If we
could honestly feel Hamlet were exaggerating in these
discourses on death, we might take some comfort in that;
we might feel the reality is not as ghastly as Hamlet's
portrayal of it, as we often feel the pessimist presents us
with a false and theoretical hopelessness, one which is distressing enough in itself but which need not apply to reality. Hamlet does just the reverse of this when he says we
will follow the outcome of the dead person "with *modesty
enough and likelihood to lead it.*" In other words, let us
trace the final disposal of the body of the great Alexander
without exaggeration and with as much likelihood as we
can fairly conjecture.

Death is the most eloquent commentary on the vanity
of life. Hamlet, who has long been cognizant of life's
weariness and staleness, here reveals his consciousness of

this in another way when he turns to contemplate death. For these thoughts are such as would proceed from such a nature as we have seen Hamlet to possess; they are not prompted solely by the occasion, i.e., an accidental chancing upon graves and bones which would bring about surmises otherwise nonexistent. The occasion inspires only the form, not the content, of Hamlet's philosophy. Horatio's "T'were to consider too curiously . . . " is the statement of a man who is as much in the presence of these things as Hamlet is, but without the inclination to glean from them the last shred of commentary on the dustiness of life. Hamlet is morbidly persistent, and in being so he does more than utter stale repetitions of what everyone knows. We are all in the presence of death in one way or another, just as the gravedigger has been; yet we may be no more concerned with it than he is. We may not laugh and joke about it as he does, but if custom has made it a property of easiness in us, we may, for all practical considerations, be taking it just as lightly. Shakespeare shows shrewd judgment in presenting first an attitude like our own, though hyperbolized to a point where we disapprove of it. If, later, we disapprove of Hamlet's attitude on the theory that it is a superfluous dramatizing of an ancient and well-recognized reality, we have merely returned to the gravedigger's state of mind. This, however, is unlikely. The sequence of Ophelia's death and then the coarse comedy of the gravediggers commits us to such a sharp repugnance toward the latter that we are almost projected into a sympathy with Hamlet when he enters and asks if this fellow has no feeling for what he is doing. The comedy is, as I said before, not softened in the least, and it continues long enough for the entry of Hamlet to be something in the nature of a relief. Momentarily we warm to the Prince's contrasting view of death, and may even follow him sympathetically as he wonders, while the clown continues to sing and toss up skulls, about these dead whose remains are so unfeelingly thrown about:

> . . . And now my Lady Worm's chapless, and knocked about
> the mazzard with a sexton's spade. Here's fine revolution, an
> we had the trick to see 't. Did these bones cost no more the
> breeding but to play at loggats with 'em? Mine ache to think
> on 't.

But these reflections, as fitting as they appear at first, begin to assume an unpalatable aspect. So long as they are confined to what is generally accepted as respect for those who have passed through the portals of death, we are at one with Hamlet; but when he persists in it, wondering about things far beyond the momentary thoughts one usually bestows upon the dead, his thoughts become disquieting. The danger of our losing sympathy with Hamlet, however, is offset by the continual singing and occasional quips of the gravedigger. The two extremes are brought into a more definite opposition when Hamlet begins to question the clown as to whose grave is being dug. Neither of them is aware that it is for Ophelia, but the audience cannot miss the high irony of the clown's continual quips and what Hamlet's reaction might be if he only knew. It is as a prelude to what he is eventually going to find out; and as the scene rises toward that mighty climax, we see him philosophizing, and not without feeling, as to the skulls of those whom he did not know. One might have been a politician, another a lawyer. Whatever they were, this horrible death-stare is what they have come to. After a few minutes, however, the gravedigger throws up the skull of someone Hamlet *has* known. It is the skull of Yorick, the King's jester. No longer is it necessary to guess what may have been the life of this grinning object; Hamlet knows, and his remarks as he takes the skull in hand become infinitely more heartfelt than were his conjectures as to those he did not know. This heart-feeling is not, however, only because he happens to have known the man; it is due also to the fact that Yorick was a "fellow of infinite jest, of most excellent fancy." He was a man of gibes, of gambols, and songs. He had "flashes of merriment that were wont to set the table on a roar." What could have been less associated with death than such a person while he lived? The appalling divergency between this grisly remnant of what once was enlivens the picture of the living man, the provoker of fun and gaiety in the King's court, the lively center of attraction amid the splendor of the King's dining table and elsewhere, always ready with a bit of foolery or a song— Hamlet enters once again into swelling scenes from the past, even if only momentarily. But they fade. And in their place is this solitary white skull against a background of darkness and silence! It has come to this! Death has triumphed over all the gaiety that has been so indifferent to Death, a thought that would overwhelm the Prince if he were only near the grave in which he knew the jester lay. How much more when he holds in his hand the horrid finality of that very head that had once been so merry, when he points to the exact place those lips used to adorn, lips he had so often kissed! "My gorge rises at it," he cannot help exclaiming. He is forced to put it down. The revulsion becomes too much for him.

But thoughts of death's irony will not leave him. After his disgust forces him to put down the skull, he wonders "to what base uses *we* may return!" The very persistence of these thoughts prolongs and explores every consideration, to the point that what seems like the climax only builds to a further intensification. How high can it go? When Hamlet's mind is thoroughly impregnated with these mounting thoughts (not *accustomed* to them, but *captured* and borne along with them), the most horrible culmination of all breaks in upon his meditations. A funeral procession enters the yard. The King and Queen are part of the procession, along with a number of courtiers and mourners. Laertes is there. The name of the deceased is not revealed for the moment, though Hamlet learns shortly when Laertes refers to his sister. This tragedy is the more paralyzing because Ophelia's death was doubtful; that is, there is a suspicion she may have taken her own life. Consequently, she is to have only a very simple funeral.

An elaborate ceremony, a grand procession that would in some way beautify the death and burial of Ophelia, this is all missing. She is simply to be committed to a hole in the earth recently dug by a clownish gravedigger. She is to become another part of that death-pile with its ironies, its awfulness, its desolation. Even she! Hamlet's "What, the fair Ophelia!" is the unbelieving gasp that escapes a soul now crushed with dread truths. Who can doubt that Hamlet reached the limit of his endurance a few moments ago when he was contemplating the skull of Yorick? Though he went further and applied its lesson to all of us in still deepening feelings, that remnant of the King's jester proved too much for him to gaze upon and he was forced to relinquish it. Hamlet's proclivity to these reflections does not bring with it the perfect equanimity necessary to gaze fixedly on death's metamorphosis in one to whom he has been so close. Yet, on top of all this and in this very place is brought the dead body of his beloved Ophelia. Love, tenderness, spiritual awareness, have combined in Hamlet to make him feel the impact of death as no one else in this scene feels it. Nor is this impact the result of one iota of artificial addition on the part of the Prince, but is due to his nature which feels a full reality where others sense it only partially. Such a sufferer may well crack, not into cowering but into rage. When Laertes leaps into the grave and bids those standing nearby to throw dust upon the living and dead together, Hamlet advances and exclaims:

> What is he whose grief
> Bears such an emphasis? Whose phrase of sorrow
> Conjures the wandering stars and makes them stand
> Like wonder-wounded hearers? This is I,
> Hamlet the Dane.

Hamlet speaks from a soul which, at that moment, will no longer contain what it bears. The great burden must be shouted, and shouted over the body of Ophelia to him who would hold that body in his arms and die with her.

Now, a rather cursory reading of this part of the scene

has led to the conclusion that Hamlet is indulging here in a bit of exhibitionism. It is maintained that he cannot bear to see Laertes proclaiming his love for his sister in front of everyone, and must needs outdo him. Indeed, if we accept the theory that Hamlet did not really love Ophelia, this is probably as good an explanation as any for the Prince's violent outburst at this point. In any event it is not a very good explanation. Not only does it make a shambles of the climax to a perfectly wrought scene of mounting significance and tension, but it makes Hamlet's conduct incomprehensible on a number of other occasions. Yet Madariaga insists that the Prince never loved Ophelia and that when he steps forward and tells how deep that love is he is simply trying to outdo Laertes; he is engaged in "a mere rivalry over passion and even over a show of passion."[8] In propounding this theory Madariaga offers as proof the fact that Hamlet, having bettered Laertes in this demonstration, never mentions Ophelia again in the play.[9] This may sound very convincing to someone only casually familiar with the text and who does not bother to check this supposed proof of Hamlet's sincerity. Let us do that first and then return to the grave of Ophelia.

There is only one scene in the play after the graveyard scene, and that final scene is taken up with matters and discussions that would make thoughts of Ophelia unlikely and certainly difficult to portray with any degree of adequacy. It begins with Hamlet telling Horatio all about his escape from death in the charge of Rosencrantz and Guildenstern. Dramatically it is necessary to let the audience know the story, but it follows quite logically from the violent reaction to the philosophical mood of the opening part of the graveyard scene. Things are moving swiftly to a crisis. Hamlet, spurred once more to the man of action, relates to his friend the recent course of events, the telling of which he was undoubtedly diverted from by the gravedigger's irreverence. This discussion is suddenly broken in upon by the appearance of Osric to announce the projected duel between Hamlet and Laertes. Osric has scarcely departed when a lord enters to find out if Hamlet is ready to fence with Laertes; he also says the King and Queen are coming right away. Hamlet then has an inexplicable foreboding of death which occasions a brief discussion between him and Laertes. The discussion is brief, however, for the duel is imminent and very shortly the King and Queen enter with all the others. The remainder of this scene is then taken up with the duel and the tragic end of so many of the principal characters. It is difficult to see any part of the entire scene wherein Hamlet ought to have mentioned Ophelia. His not mentioning her is no proof that his behavior at the grave was mere sham.

Madariaga further stipulates that when Hamlet first learns at the grave that the dead person is Ophelia, his "What, the fair Ophelia!" is cold. "This 'fair', which he has already used in another occasion, formal and indifferent, underlines the coldness with which he learns the death of the young woman."[10] I frankly do not see this at all. The lines could be rendered coldly or passionately, depending upon the interpretation of Hamlet's state of mind at this moment, but to insist arbitrarily that the word itself is cold and must be given coldly, and then to conclude that Hamlet is therefore cold about Ophelia's death, need hardly be taken seriously.

Yet, even if we agree that Hamlet truly loved Ophelia and that her death was the more shocking to him because of his state of mind just prior to the appearance of her funeral procession, his emotional outburst at her grave may still appear strange. If it does there are other things that may help to explain it. We must continue to see the pattern we have found so many times made evident in these emotional changes. "The fair Ophelia!" is not the cold thing Madariaga would have it, nor is Hamlet's use of this expression on a previous occasion cold, as the same writer insists. In the past the fair Ophelia has been, to Hamlet, in marked contrast to the unweeded garden. So is she now in marked contrast to the hideous death realm we have just witnessed. In both cases this contrast turns out to be false. First she proved really very much a part of the world Hamlet loathes, much to his utter chagrin, and the emotional reaction in Hamlet was violent. It was more than a disappointment in love. It was the tarnishing of an angel. But now, that the fair Ophelia could become a part of the thing that makes Hamlet's gorge rise is a phenomenon which, however we must accept it as true sooner or later, becomes too much for the weaker part of Hamlet's human nature. Both disappointments, though common enough in this life, become unbearable when a beloved ideal is identified with what we despise in life and with what horrifies us in death. Each is a tragedy in its own way. But the latter is a tragedy beyond reclamation or recall, and one which, in the present case, touches swiftly home when the Queen says

> I hoped thou shouldst have been my Hamlet's wife,
> I thought thy bride bed to have decked, sweet maid,
> And not have strewed thy grave.

It is the first time in the play that one of those in power expresses a wish that Hamlet and Ophelia had found happiness together—after it is too late!

Whatever Hamlet might think upon this is rudely interrupted when Laertes curses him whose wicked deed deprived Ophelia of her "most ingenious sense." It may be wondered just how exactly Hamlet comprehends Laertes, that is, whether he understands Laertes to accuse him of depriving her of her life or of her reason. The words could convey either. Hamlet was away when Ophelia went mad, but it is quite probable Horatio told him of it on his return. In either sense the words would be bound to provoke Hamlet. To the eye of the world which sees only the bare fact of Hamlet's having slain her father and so, indirectly, caused Ophelia's death, this fiery speech of Laertes seems defensible enough. The facts are appallingly true. There is another side to all this, however, which the others have never even suspected, not even from his first love for Ophelia. There is no evidence that any of them took it seriously, prior to the belatedly expressed hope by the Queen, to say nothing of having any appreciation of what this love really meant to the Prince. Polonius's belief that love drove him mad we can dismiss utterly. All were glib and sure, and they were wrong. But appearances are against Hamlet, and this is more galling than if Laertes' speech were a complete fabrication and not likely to be believed. The facts are indisputably there. Except Horatio, no one knows of the circumstances surrounding the accidental slaying of Polonius—the fact that all secrets were uncovered between the murderous King and Hamlet, and suspicious movements behind the arras were fraught with menace. They know little of the Prince's mental turmoil which has increased rather than lessened, right to the combination of the present scene and the revelation of Ophelia's death. Hamlet hears himself not only denounced but cursed as the author of this woe, and cursed before those who undoubtedly believe him to be guilty.

Is the Prince provoked to an outburst by this? Small wonder if he were. But there is one further incident that puts Hamlet out of all control. Laertes leaps into the grave and takes Ophelia in his arms. Then he bids that dirt be thrown on both of them that he and his sister may be joined in the grave:

> Now pile your dust upon the quick and dead
> Till of this flat a mountain you have made
> To o'ertop old Pelion or the skyish head
> Of blue Olympus.

On top of his cursing Hamlet he makes this demonstration of his own love for Ophelia by way of contrast. Hamlet is the author of her death; he, Laertes, would willingly die with her. It is then that Hamlet steps forward demanding to know who can grieve more than he over the death of Ophelia. Rather than question the sincerity of Hamlet here, I think it far more to the point to question the sincerity of Laertes. There is no doubt that he loves his sister and is grief-stricken at her untimely death. But his leaping into the grave and demanding to be buried with her must certainly appear to many readers like an exaggerated performance, whether the exaggeration be due to a desire to demonstrate how grief-stricken he is, or to an excess of emotion in the passionate young man. The latter is more likely and better fits the character as we see it in action elsewhere. Nevertheless, even a thing said in passion and which seems like the truth at the time it is said, cannot be accepted as really intended, particularly if we wish to make a test of consulting the person when he is in a calmer frame of mind. In the early part of the play when we see Laertes and Ophelia together we do not get any evidence of extraordinary affection between the two. They give every appearance of being a normal brother-and-sister pair. Laertes has been in France, has returned to Denmark to do his duty to the coronation of Claudius, and that being done he is more than anxious to be off once more to France. He says nothing that would imply his return to Denmark was anything more than courtesy to his king. There is no evidence that he was happy at being re-united with his father and sister, or that he is the least bit sorrowful over leaving them again. His taking leave of Ophelia is cordial, not affectionate. Their last few moments together are taken up almost wholly with Laertes' advice about how Ophelia should conduct herself with Hamlet; she must be careful of her chastity and believe the Prince only so far as he backs his promises with deeds. It is good advice, of course, but given in the deliberate language of one who might be advising almost anyone. It hardly proceeds from a warm love. Laertes says nothing about her happiness being his happiness, or that any harm that might befall her would greatly concern him because of the deep love he bears her. Elsewhere he tells her to be sure to write to him; and when the time comes for him to be gone he says simply, "Farewell, Ophelia, and remember well what I have said to you." Nothing in this entire scene could possibly induce us to believe that Laertes could not go on living if anything should happen to his sister.

We must also keep in mind that when Laertes returns from France and learns from the King that Hamlet is responsible for the death of Polonius, he says, in so many words, that revenge is the uppermost thought in his mind.

> . . . let him come.
> It warms the very sickness in my heart
> That I shall live and tell him to his teeth
> "Thus didest thou."

This passion for revenge is expressed several times by Laertes, and it is a little difficult to reconcile with his desire to die in the grave with Ophelia before this revenge is accomplished. Unless, as I have said, we look upon his action at the grave as an impassioned and somewhat thoughtless deed. It is a logical assumption. He has lost his father and soon afterward he has lost his sister. The double tragedy has had its effect, and now the simple burial of his sister aggravates him to the point where he tells the attending priest

> I tell thee, churlish priest,
> A ministering angel shall my sister be
> When thou liest howling.

This, even though the priest is not personally responsible. Laertes' behavior is understandable, perhaps, but not a true expression of what is and is not so. After he and Hamlet have grappled with each other and been parted by the others, Laertes says not another word; nor does he attempt to get back into the grave.

Now, we have traced the state of mind of Hamlet right to this point, as well as the probable reaction to Laertes cursing him. Add to this the obvious exaggeration in Laertes' profession of love and I think we can understand why Hamlet comes forth and challenges the other to any demonstration of love and so decide who loved Ophelia more. It may be objected that Hamlet could not have been aware of these things that militate against Laertes' desire to die with his sister. He was not on hand when Laertes was bidding Ophelia farewell in Act I, Sc. iii, and he has no direct knowledge of Laertes' vow to revenge his father's death. No, this is quite true. And even if he did know of these things the chances are he would not be mulling them over in the graveyard. But he did know Laertes. And just as any of us can instinctively recognize false or exaggerated behavior in a person we have known for a long time, without consciously enumerating all past actions which would render the present one different, so Hamlet (who, as we have seen, shows an extraordinary ability to see through people) could easily see in a flash that Laertes, who met the Queen's sentiments with a curse, is indulging in something which does not ring true. What if Hamlet has not actually witnessed the farewell between Laertes and Ophelia? He must have seen other things and been well aware of what this scene indicates.

Brooding, anguished, stunned by tragedy, cursed, inflamed beyond all patience, Hamlet springs toward the grave of Ophelia. He becomes like Laertes himself; indeed, he gets the better of the other man. It is one more time when Hamlet ceases to be the man of angel soul and becomes the raging lion.

> I prithee, take thy fingers from my throat,
> For though I am not splenitive and rash,
> Yet have I in me something dangerous,
> Which let thy wisdom fear. Hold off thy hand.

As for his own love for Ophelia,

> I loved Ophelia. Forty thousand brothers
> Could not, with all their quantity of love,
> Make up my sum. What wilt thou do for her?

> 'Swounds, show me what thou'lt do.
> Woo't weep? Woo't fight? Woo't fast? Woo't tear thyself?

Woo't drink up eisel? Eat a crocodile?
I'll do 't.

He speaks with raging scorn of what, to him, is mere rant on the part of Laertes:

> Dost thou come here to whine?
> To outface me with leaping in her grave?
> Be buried quick with her, and so will I.
> And if thou prate of mountains, let them throw
> Millions of acres on us, till our ground,
> Singeing his pate against the burning zone,
> Make Ossa like a wart! Nay, an thou 'lt mouth,
> I'll rant as well as thou.

Through all this Laertes says nothing. And it is strange that he remains silent. Here is a man whose passion when aroused seems uncontrollable; a man who has braved his monarch to his face with "O thou vile King," and "to Hell, allegiance!" a man who is being challenged and taunted by the very one who slew his father and caused his sister's death, and whom he has vowed to kill. Yet he has not a word to say, not even to Hamlet's parting shot,

> Let Hercules himself do what he may,
> The cat will mew and dog will have his day.

Can it be that something about Hamlet overpowers him at that moment? Laertes is no coward, nor is it likely that he is controlling himself, under such circumstances, to insure the plot he and the King have devised. Both King and Queen plead with Laertes to be patient, but such pleadings have had small effect in the past when his passion was up, and I do not think these two are keeping him calm now. He is not calm, as a matter of fact; he was not so a few moments ago and nothing has happened to calm him down meanwhile. He is smoldering and glowering at the affronts of his hated enemy. The truth is that the surprising outburst in the ordinarily calm Hamlet has caused a similar, though opposite, change in Laertes. He has met his match, and in a decidedly unlooked-for quarter. It is a psychological reaction very often seen when an opponent who should be a weakling turns out to be a wildcat. Hamlet meets Laertes head on, defies him, dares him, sneers at him. And Laertes, glaring back at him, holds his peace. Those who read Hamlet's vituperation as mere show have not a very probable opinion of what the impassioned Laertes is forced to respect. Hamlet's behavior may be unexpected and it may seem inexplicable to those who are oblivious of the reasons for it, but it is hardly theatrical. The full impact of his outfacing Laertes rests entirely on Hamlet's absolute sincerity, his earnest anger which Laertes feels the brunt of and which is perhaps the only thing that could subdue Laertes into the belief that his wish to die with his sister was not so real after all.

This entire scene, undeniably gripping all the way through, is but a further confirmation of Hamlet's character as we have seen it revealed in other places. What happens needs only to be seen clearly for it to be related to the rest of the play. Hamlet's changes of temperament are entirely logical and fit right into place, for all that they are misunderstood by some of those about him. These have misunderstood him before because, in this scene as in others, they fail to see properly, and not because there is anything essentially strange in Hamlet. We have seen his love for Ophelia in its true light. We have seen the burden of duty under which he labors. We have followed his thoughts on the skulls in the graveyard. Except for his friend Horatio, none of the others sees Hamlet's actions in this scene as the direct consequence of all these things, and the Queen's "This is mere madness" is as ill founded as it was when she pronounced him mad because he saw a ghost she could not see.

Nowhere else in the play does Shakespeare so vividly bring out a weakness that only the good can be guilty of, as well as the failure of society to construe the behavior occasioned by this weakness. If Hamlet had been a different person his deportment might have been something we could designate as socially acceptable. As it is we know it is occasioned by that weakness peculiar to near-perfection. To those all about him it is incomprehensible, but the incessant pronouncement of "madness" at Hamlet's every turn is only the cry of a myopic-visioned world grown too accustomed to seeing itself as the center of all things. Hamlet faces life as a problematical reality, in contrast to a materialistic society that pursues smooth and attractive nonentities.*

---

*The question of Hamlet's age is one I do not pretend to be able to settle. Since the gravedigger refers in this scene (lines 163-178 *passim*) to Hamlet's birth as having been thirty years ago, all of us who believe the Prince to be a much younger man are hard put to reconcile his youth with the gravedigger's calculations. If a mature and experienced man like Iago is only twenty-eight, Hamlet, whose love Laertes describes as a "violet in the youth of primy nature," can hardly be two years Iago's senior. All the discussion over the age of Hamlet proves simply that we have abundant reason for thinking him much younger. Otherwise we would accept him as thirty and let it go at that. It is just possible that the clownish gravedigger is mistaken and Hamlet is too pre-occupied at the moment to correct him. Or it may be a mistake in the text, even though Yorick, who bore Hamlet on his back a thousand times, has lain in the earth "three and twenty years." If Hamlet's age were a printer's error, the number of years Yorick has been dead might have been altered deliberately. Two errors are as possible as one.

VII

HAMLET RAGES

During the course of the play there are three times
when Hamlet becomes thoroughly aroused. The first time
is when Ophelia returns his gifts and he reacts by treating her so brutally. The second time is when he reproaches
the Queen in her room at night directly after the performance of the play. And the third is by the grave of Ophelia.
We have seen that his actions on these occasions proceed
from his state of mind as conditioned by attendant circumstances, and we have seen also that even these variables
are consistent; they confirm rather than contradict or
weaken our impression of the Prince. However, there is

more to it than this. There is a special connection among these three instances, quite apart from their obvious similarity, which makes them more significant than would be the case if they were nothing more than unrelated incidents enabling us to see when and why Hamlet's ire is up and what he is like when this happens.

It is Hamlet's duty to punish evil—this is his major concern. But evil, while we find it in many quarters and in varying degrees of culpability, is represented in the play chiefly by three persons: the King, the Queen, and Laertes. The King represents deliberate evil, consciously planned and executed; the Queen represents evil which is the result of weakness, specifically the weakness of the flesh; Laertes represents evil that is the consequence of uncontrolled passion, not the passion of desire as in the case of the Queen, but the passion for revenge and retaliation. Both weakness and uncontrolled passion in the personages of those who represent them come under the influence of deliberate evil, and are tempted and abetted in the commission of further wrongs. The King is the instigator or fountainhead of evil, but while he is the most guilty of the three this does not absolve the other two. He can draw them into wrongdoing by means of their cooperation with him and in no other way, and they must bear their guilt insofar as they are responsible for whatever misdeeds they commit. Nevertheless, Hamlet has been expressly ordered to punish the evil source, the King, and to leave the Queen to heaven and her own conscience. We do not think of Gertrude or Laertes as wicked even though their sins can be named. Yet it is against the Queen and Laertes that Hamlet becomes most easily wrought up, whereas he cannot bring himself to any punitive measures with regard to Claudius. The Queen's weakness and resultant sin have existed from before the beginning of the play, while Laertes' actions come as a result of Hamlet's departure from his mission of justice and from his momentary recklessness while so doing. The stabbing of Polonius sets forces in motion which, with the help of the unprincipled King whom Hamlet has neglected, rebound against the Prince. This is, in a certain sense, retribution for having forsaken a clearly appointed course and strayed elsewhere against specific instructions to the contrary. While the slaying of Polonius has all the appearances of an unfortunate accident, its very fortuity only emphasizes the misdirected rage of the Prince during a period of willful omission from which nothing good results. The Queen is not rescued from sin, another potential evil is precipitated, and the King, far from having been dealt retributive justice, is given another fertile field in which to exercise his evil genius. Things are worse than they were before, despite the fact that Hamlet has apparently set out to reform his wayward mother and bring her back to the path of virtue. He has done two wrongs, first in neglecting the greater wrong for the lesser, and second in committing a rash deed.

The wrong he is doing, however, is not apparent to him as he comes to his mother's room and denounces her for her unworthy life with Claudius. Hamlet is so carried away as he empties all his pent-up malediction upon her that he does not stop to think clearly of what he is saying or what desirable end he hopes to achieve by saying it. The effect on her is one of unbearable devastation:

> O Hamlet, speak no more.
> Thou turn'st mine eyes into my very soul,
> And there I see such black and grained spots
> As will not leave their tinct.

The effect seems for the moment to be a good one. The Queen in being made aware of her transgressions is, we would think, at least on her way to repentance and betterment. But here the ghost enters, bids Hamlet desist, speaks of his almost blunted purpose, and tells him to go comfort his mother. Every word of the ghost's very brief admonition is a pointed, almost scathing repetition of what he said to Hamlet that night on the platform. The Prince has fallen into something very wrong, even though he appears to be saying here and now what is the positive truth. Now, it does not require any extended treatment to dismiss such possibilities as that the ghost absolves or condones Gertrude, or that Hamlet's self-righteousness is wrong in itself. There is no question of the Queen's guilt, and if Hamlet is wrong it is not because he is confronting her with it. In the first place Hamlet's language to the Queen is excessive, certainly, right up to the point where he is dissuaded by the ghost. There is not a trace of gentleness in his remonstrances; indeed, he goes into unnecessary and disgusting detail as he rants the facts of her sex life at her. He is harsh and cruel even though he may be morally correct. Three times she begs him to stop, but he is not the least softened, and from the sudden breaking off after "A king of shreds and patches—" at the entry of the ghost, the indication is he would have continued further. From the very beginning the Queen is amazed at her son's demeanor. At first she fears he will kill her and she screams for help. A little later she says

> What have I done that thou darest wag thy tongue
> In noise so rude against me?

Still later,

> Aye me, what act
> That roars so loud and thunders in the index?

Is this raging man the same Hamlet we have pronounced to be of angel soul? From Gertrude's reaction it is easy to see that such ferocity is unusual, if not altogether unknown, in her son. What makes him so harsh and cruel to his own mother even after she begs him several times to spare her? The question can be answered only by reverting to the subject of whether the motive be inclination or duty. Is Hamlet speaking here from personal spleen or from outraged morality? The two are often difficult to distinguish, so much so that one is frequently confused with the other. An honest detestation of sin is very often thought to be—and summarily dismissed as being—nothing but personal pique. And just as often do high sounding condemnations proceed from nothing more than intense dislike or personal discomfort. There is no easy trick for determining whether it is one or the other, for an individual may not even guess his own motives properly, much less those of another. Only by the deepest introspection, and sometimes not even then, can he come to some degree of certainty as to just why he condemns the actions of someone else. As personal feelings guide Laertes' sense of honor (rather than the other way round), so personal feelings guide Hamlet's sense of moral virtue in this particular scene. In each case an essentially good quality becomes misdirected, and its net results are far more likely to be bad than good because the proper hierarchy of virtues is upset.

This is proved by the slaying of Polonius, an act committed in the very state of mind Hamlet is in from the time he enters the Queen's closet till he sees the ghost. The stabbing of the old man is no extrinsic act gratuitously included in a scene devoted to the denunciation of Gertrude by her son, but an ample demonstration of the deranged state of Hamlet at that moment. It is further proved by everything Hamlet says in condemning his mother. There is not a word about her adultery, her hasty re-marriage, or the canon laws against such a marriage. Yet we might expect Hamlet to make these things his principal theme, particularly in view of the religious tone with which he commences. When the Queen asks what she has done that he should raise his voice so rudely against her, Hamlet replies:

> Such an act
> That blurs the grace and blush of modesty,
> Calls virtue hypocrite, takes off the rose
> From the fair forehead of an innocent love,
> And sets a blister there—makes marriage vows
> As false as dicers' oaths. Oh, such a deed
> As from the body of contraction plucks
> The very soul, and sweet religion makes
> A rhapsody of words. Heaven's face doth glow,

> Yea, this solidity and compound mass,
> With tristful visage, as against the doom,
> Is thought-sick at the act.

All this is quite true. The Queen has indeed made sweet religion "a rhapsody of words," but the reasons why are not those which Hamlet gives. His entire argument rests on a comparison of the personal attributes of the elder Hamlet and Claudius, how her first husband was so much better than her second that there is in fact no comparison:

> Look here upon this picture, and on this,
> The counterfeit presentment of two brothers.
> See what a grace was seated on this brow—
> Hyperion's curls, the front of Jove himself,
> An eye like Mars, to threaten and command,
> A station like the herald Mercury
> New-lighted on a heaven-kissing hill,
> A combination and a form indeed
> Where every god did seem to set his seal
> To give the world assurance of a man.
> This was your husband. Look you now what follows.
> Here is your husband, like a mildewed ear,
> Blasting his wholesome brother. Have you eyes?
> Could you on this fair mountain leave to feed
> And batten on this moor? Ha! Have you eyes?
> You cannot call it love, for at your age
> The heyday in the blood is tame, it's humble,
> And waits upon the judgment. And what judgment
> Would step from this to this? Sense sure you have,
> Else could you not have motion. But sure that sense
> Is apoplexed; for madness would not err,
> Nor sense to ecstasy was ne'er so thralled
> But it reserved some quantity of choice
> To serve in such a difference. What devil was 't
> That thus hath cozened you at hoodman-blind?
> Eyes without feeling, feeling without sight,
> Ears without hands or eyes, smelling sans all,
> Or but a sickly part of one true sense
> Could not so mope.

Her crime, if we follow Hamlet's line of reasoning, consists in having married such a poor specimen of manhood after having been wed to a paragon. How could she have done such a thing? We may wonder, as Hamlet does. But however we may condemn her poor choice in a second husband, we can hardly think it an act "that blurs the grace and blush of modesty," or that it "calls virtue hypocrite." It does not bear out any of the descriptions Hamlet gives of her deed. Nor is it any more to the point that he calls the King a murderer and a villain and so characterizes him as an actual criminal, for, from every bit of evidence we can glean, Claudius is solely responsible for the murder. It is his crime, not hers, and the fact that she married a villain deserves far less reproach than the actual transgressions she has committed and for which she is answerable.

From this evident discrepancy between what Hamlet starts to say and what he ends up by saying, it is fairly clear that he speaks from feelings he does not fully understand. But having posed the question as to whether Hamlet's impulse is a moral or a personal one, we are still faced with the problem, if we choose the latter, of deciding precisely what the personal impulse is. Too often a question of this kind is argued between the most extreme alternatives. It is either wholly moral or wholly worldly. Either Hamlet is being scrupulously religious in his condemnation of his mother's actions, or he is speaking from motives (perhaps not consciously understood by himself) that are completely without any religious or moral basis whatever. And if it can be demonstrated that the moral basis is lacking, or at least that it is not entirely consonant with the accusations Hamlet flings at the Queen, the alternative theory is presumed to be proved by default. Hamlet is a self-righteous hypocrite, or he has the Oedipus complex. Now, I maintain that we wander further from the answer than ever if we attempt anything like this. All such theories have a very farfetched sound to begin with, and the more we examine them the more vulnerable they become, with the result that they must be continually bolstered by dragging in notions not supported by any evidence (direct or inferential) in the play. I have deliberately used the word *personal* rather than *selfish* in describing what I believe to be Hamlet's real motive in this scene. If I were to use the second word I would not use it in the sense of greedy or avaricious, but simply in a materialistic sense, and I would apply it to Hamlet in order to designate him as a person whose real stimuli are always worldly, whether conscious or subconscious. I would regard this selfish Hamlet as the real Hamlet and all his shocked morality as a veneer spread upon burning resentment over material disappointments. Having gone that far and being asked to name these disappointments, I would have to strike around and then come up with such things as his being deprived of the throne and—at least to a certain extent—the love of his mother. Hamlet would have to be shown as the kind of person who desires these things keenly or they would not cause him to be so thoroughly aroused at being deprived of them, and consequently he would be an ardent materialist regarding the one and greedy for material affection as to the other.

Now, Hamlet's desire for the crown, while he does mention it a number of times during the course of the play, has, to my mind, been vastly overrated by many. Neither in the first soliloquy nor in his long conversation with Horatio (Act I, Sc. iv) in which he speaks of the present faults of the Danish people does he say a word about it. Nothing is said about it either during or after the conversation with the ghost in the next scene, the matter of which uncovers evidence which fully disqualifies Claudius as rightful king. Still later, Rosencrantz suggests to Hamlet that thwarted ambition may be the cause of his melancholy, but Hamlet replies with what amounts to a specific denial:

> Oh, God, I could be bounded in a nutshell and count myself
> a king of infinite space were it not that I have bad dreams.

This is said before he even suspects that Rosencrantz and Guildenstern are anything but his good friends. It is Guildenstern who presses the idea with

Hamlet's further comments, while they may be tortured into some kind of concurrence that he is ambitious, are too lacking in any kind of vehemence to imply that he burns to be King of Denmark. When he tells Rosencrantz after the play that he lacks advancement he is only echoing what his no longer trustworthy friend has already said to him, and he says it, moreover, to throw the snooping Rosencrantz off the track. All these instances, together with Hamlet's remark to the King just before the play, and his mentioning to Horatio (Act V, Sc. ii) that Claudius has

> Popped in between the election and my hopes

do not build a very convincing case for Hamlet's political frustration. It does exist, undoubtedly, but in a decidedly secondary way when compared with other disappointments of a less material order. Even Hamlet's remarks to Rosencrantz and Guildenstern about his being a beggar and being most dreadfully attended are prompted more by his inability to entertain his friends adequately, than by any personal fondness for royal comfort. To attempt to read his motives elsewhere in the light of a kind of justifiable worldliness here, demands a great amount of fetching into empty places for evidence.

The plain and simple fact is that if Hamlet sorely desired the throne he would say so. He does not, nor can any of his spiritual sufferings be construed as subconscious desires masked under the guise of virtuous inclining. Respecting Hamlet's relationship to Gertrude, though various interpretations may be more arguable, the case against selfishness of any kind is just as conclusive. I have already attempted to show this in studying Hamlet's first soliloquy; what is true there is no less true here. He speaks to his mother from the hurt she has done him, but it is a hurt done to his personal and spiritual nature rather than a grosser wound inflicted by the transfer of her affections to Claudius. In the first place Claudius's short-comings and his downright wickedness, while they are substantially different from the wrong Gertrude has committed in marrying him, are not so thoroughly disconnected from it as to justify our seeking far-flung explanations why Hamlet mentions one and not the other. When the ghost first visited Hamlet and revealed the murder and the Queen's adultery, he said, among other things:

> Aye, that incestuous, that adulterate beast,
> With witchcraft of his wit, with traitorous gifts—
> O wicked wit and gifts, that have the power
> So to seduce!—won to his shameful lust
> The will of my most seeming-virtuous Queen.
> O Hamlet, what a falling-off was there!
> From me, whose love was of that dignity
> That it went hand in hand even with the vow
> I made to her in marriage, and to decline
> Upon a wretch whose natural gifts were poor
> To those of mine!
> But virtue, as it never will be moved
> Though lewdness court it in a shape of Heaven,
> So lust, though to a radiant angel linked,
> Will sate itself in a celestial bed
> And prey on garbage.

These utterances are virtually the same as what Hamlet says when denouncing his mother, and the point to bear in mind is that this twice-expressed castigation of both Claudius and Gertrude is absolutely true. It is not a fiction conjured up in a mind warped by personal jealousy or disappointed ambition. Even at the very height of Hamlet's passionate denunciation we cannot find so much as a syllable that would not square with what the ghost has said and with what is substantiated by the facts that come to light. Uncontrolled though the Prince may be he speaks only the truth:

> A murderer and a villain,
> A slave that is not twentieth part the tithe
> Of your precedent lord, a vice of kings,
> A cutpurse of the empire and the rule,

That from a shelf the precious diadem stole
And put it in his pocket!

The utmost criticism we could level at this would be to call it hyperbolical. But so is the language of the ghost, and unless ghosts be also supposed to suffer from subconscious emotions, the language is justified.

Now, the factuality of what Hamlet says cannot be dismissed on the ground that it is beside the point. That is to say, it may be conceded that Hamlet is correct enough in what he says of Claudius without altering in any way his reason for saying it. If he were motivated by a sense of alienation of his mother's love, and thereby prompted to scathing denunciation of the man responsible, would it necessarily follow that he would falsify or exaggerate the other man's faults? Is it not just possible he would have an eye only for faults that do not exist, even though he is prompted to be critical by feelings of jealousy? Of course it is possible. However, I am not discussing possibilities and impossibilities, but probabilities. I want to interpret this scene on the basis of what the evidence points to and what fits the play as a whole, not anything and everything that *could be*. Admit all remote possibilities and there is no limit to what the play may mean.

It is possible, but *extremely unlikely*, that Hamlet's catalogue of the King's defects would proceed from a jealous brain, and yet be thoroughly consistent with the facts, particularly in the uncontrollable state the Prince is obviously in. Some inconsistency would show itself. I made the point heretofore that, though the first soliloquy is critical of Claudius and Gertrude, there are no false accusations in it. Hamlet says nothing beyond what is actually known to him at the time, and while the soliloquy itself is bitter, it is not intemperate. It is only after the ghost's revelation that Hamlet refers to Claudius as a "smiling, damned villain." This present scene takes place right after the performance of the play which confronted

197

both Claudius and Gertrude with their guilty behavior. Even though Hamlet indulged in a few moments of escapism directly afterward, he did, as I said, return to what the play conclusively proved, and he stands now with all the evidence he needs. If he is more violent than he has ever been in the past his violence is due partly to the fact that there is no longer any conceivable doubt. Where, at any point in the play, do we find the slightest indication that Hamlet's condemnation of his uncle is excessive? It grows in direct ratio with what he finds out and what he proves.

Hamlet says nothing of Claudius, therefore, that would imply concerns that are unjustifiable or extrinsic to what he, Hamlet, should be about. But the points on which he seems at odds with his mission are first, that he levels all his ire at his mother instead of Claudius himself, and second, that he makes the comparison between his father and his uncle the principal theme of what he says whereas the ghost only mentions it in passing. Hamlet confines himself to one phase of what should be his total undertaking, and he confronts the accomplice instead of the wrongdoer. I have spoken before of one particular weakness of Hamlet's idealism lying in the fact that he is more desirous of the rewards of idealism than its unpleasant duties. By the same token he is more sensitive to the pains of a lost idealism than he is alive to a more comprehensive difference between right and wrong. The weakness is consistent in that it is always personal with Hamlet. That is why he is moved to such violent action in certain quarters while remaining so strangely apathetic in others. We are perfectly correct in seeing that Hamlet's idealism is too personal to be broad enough for the absolute ideal, but utterly wrong when we imagine his personal feelings have nothing at all to do with that ideal. The wrong done becomes personalized through the medium of his mother. Had this been accidental, Hamlet's treatment of her would be unpardonable. But she has lent her willing cooperation to Claudius and linked Hamlet to a racking situation. She has left a celestial height and entered a dank pit, not only entered it but tenderly embraced its lord with whom she has forced Hamlet into a filial relationship. These things are not so grave as the crimes committed by her husband, but they are what most directly affects Hamlet. The resulting hurt is one of the spirit, a consciousness of the ugliness of clearly discernible corruptions, the "honeying and making love over a nasty sty." It is not a worldly disadvantage incidental to the wrong, but the sharp point of the wrong itself.

As virtue attracts the idealist, so sin repels. Moralists as well as amoralists tend to forget that. The one dwells too much on what he rightly calls the "false" beauties of sin, the other on what he mistakenly believes to be sin's true beauty. But it is the amoralist who refuses to admit such a thing as an honest revulsion to immorality where, in a social sense, everything else seems to be agreeable enough. For this is the thing Hamlet feels, but he feels it most strongly where the impact is greatest. Though Gertrude is but an accomplice and Claudius committed the chief crime, it is she who stands accusably an agent without which Claudius might never have wrought such evil. Only the basest lust could have caused her to play such a role. But the judgment we must inevitably arrive at is that Hamlet is acting from a sense of discomfort to himself, however spiritual it is, and he is verbally punishing a sinner while neglecting her corrupter, however legitimate he may be in his accusations. It is an indignation misplaced. Only the ghostly monitor can halt him and urge his gentle exhortation, "Speak to her, Hamlet."

The unforseeable concatenation of tragic consequences that stems from the killing of Polonius includes the death of Ophelia and the vengeance of Laertes which itself brings death to many more people. Now, this vengeance and its dire results have certain aspects that deserve to be examined, inasmuch as there is a decided change which comes over Laertes between the time we first see him demanding to know who killed his father and the time when he is mortally wounded and asks Hamlet's forgiveness. In the previous chapter we saw the beginning of that change when Hamlet and Laertes clashed head on at Ophelia's grave. To appreciate its full import, however, we would do well to view a little more closely Laertes' varying states of mind before and after this all-important brawl that appears to have such a profound effect upon him.

In Act IV, Sc. v, when Laertes bursts in upon the King to demand an explanation for the death and obscure funeral of Polonius, the young man is so wrought up and unmanageable that it appears beyond the King's power to calm him. This is first conveyed when there is a tumult outside and a gentleman hurries in to advise the King to save himself:

> Save yourself, my lord.
> The ocean, overpeering of his list,
> Eats not the flats with more impetuous haste
> Than young Laertes, in a riotous head,
> O'erbears your officers. The rabble call him lord,
> And as the world were now but to begin,
> Antiquity forgot, custom not known,
> The ratifiers and props of every word,
> They cry "Choose we—Laertes shall be King!"
> Caps, hands, and tongues applaud it to the clouds—
> "Laertes shall be King, Laertes King!"

A few seconds later the outer doors are broken and Laertes rushes in followed by a band of Danes. "O thou vile King," he roars, "give me my father!" In response to the Queen's "Calmly, good Laertes," he snaps back

> That drop of blood that's calm proclaims me bastard,
> Cries cuckold to my father, brands the harlot
> Even here, between the chaste unsmirched brows
> Of my true mother.

The King asks Laertes what is the cause of this rebellion and why he is so incensed, not as if he, the King, did not know perfectly well, but in an attempt to bring Laertes to a more reasonable frame of mind and so listen to the answers he is demanding. Laertes' only reply is to roar out, "Where is my father?"

KING.   Dead.
QUEEN.   But not by him.
KING.   Let him demand his fill.
LAERTES.   How came he dead? I'll not be juggled with.
                To Hell, allegiance! Vows, to the blackest devil!
                Conscience and grace, to the profoundest pit!
                I dare damnation. To this point I stand,
                That both the worlds I give to negligence.
                Let come what comes, only I'll be revenged
                Most throughly for my father.
KING.   Who shall stay you?
LAERTES.   My will, not all the world.
                And for my means, I'll husband them so well
                They shall go far with little.
KING.   Good Laertes,
                If you desire to know the certainty
                Of your dear father's death, is 't writ in your
                    revenge
                That, swoopstake, you will draw both friend
                    and foe,
                Winner and loser?
LAERTES.   None but his enemies.
KING.   Will you know them, then?
LAERTES.   To his good friends thus wide I'll ope my arms,
                And like the kind life-rendering pelican,
                Repast them with my blood.
KING.   Why, now you speak
                Like a good child and a true gentleman.
                That I am guiltless of your father's death,
                And am most sensibly in grief for it,
                It shall as level to your judgment pierce
                As day does to your eye.

Claudius is not patient and understanding in this instance; his manner is one of weakness. Despite the fact that he is innocent of the death of Polonius there is no royal resentment at Laertes' fury. On the contrary, the King behaves as one who dares not oppose this dangerous person or even appear to be differing with him in the slightest, but who must somehow convey to him the unreasonableness of wreaking vengeance on friend and foe alike. When the uproar was heard outside, the King's first thought was for his own safety. "Where are my Switzers?" he asked. "Let them guard the door." Furthermore, the King is not being wily now in the sense that he sees Laertes as a ready instrument to turn against Hamlet. So far as the King knows, Hamlet is already being dispatched in England. It is not until two scenes later that he receives the letter informing him that Hamlet is back in Denmark, after which he begins to help Laertes plot Hamlet's death. The only danger the King apprehends at this point is from Laertes himself, and in attempting to avoid that danger Claudius resorts to a conciliatory manner that goes beyond whatever sympathy we can suppose an impenitent fratricide to be capable of. The hypocrisy of the following lines is rather obvious:

> Laertes, I must commune with your grief,
> Or you deny me right. Go but apart,
> Make choice of whom your wisest friends you will,
> And they shall hear and judge 'twixt you and me.
> If by direct or by collateral hand
> They find us touched, we will our kingdom give,
> Our crown, our life, and all that we call ours,
> To you in satisfaction. But if not,
> Be you content to lend your patience to us
> And we shall jointly labor with your soul
> To give it due content.

The King's feelings either for Polonius or for Laertes, are hardly so personal as to prompt a desire to "commune" with the young man's grief. Back in Act IV, Sc. i, when the Queen first told him of Hamlet's killing Polonius, Claudius was less concerned over the death of his chief counsellor than over his own narrow escape and the possibility that the murder might be charged to him:

> It had been so with us had we been there.
> His liberty is full of threats to all,
> To you yourself, to us, to everyone.
> Alas, how shall this bloody deed be answered?

> It will be laid to us, whose providence
> Should have kept short, restrained and out of haunt,
> This mad young man.

Now, Laertes is deaf to any soothing influence which proceeds so obviously from timidity. It is true that he finally becomes pacified but only when he is convinced that the King was in no way responsible for the death of Polonius. Never does the royal authority assert itself against the treasonable utterances of Laertes, nor, once Laertes becomes convinced of the King's innocence, does he render apologies for having defied him. He is shown to be a thoroughly overriding and headstrong young man whose sense of accord with others depends entirely upon how he happens to feel. While his spleen is not so uncontrollable as to vent itself upon innocent persons it is uncontrolled nevertheless, and Laertes is now in that dangerously calm frame of mind that will soon lend itself to the King's dastardly plots. When the letter arrives telling that Hamlet has landed in Denmark "naked and alone," the natures of these two men are fairly bound to fall into quick conspiracy. But the King, who feels his own safety depends on Hamlet being killed as quickly as possible, realizes he must touch off the hot-tempered Laertes in the very way that proved so unstoppable a short time before:

> Laertes, was your father dear to you?
> Or are you like the painting of a sorrow,
> A face without a heart?

Knowing himself to be safe from Laertes and in danger from Hamlet, the King's ready recourse is to incense Laertes once again as an immediate instrument of murder. Not only does he refer to what will accomplish the desired reaction, but he does it in such a way as to insinuate that if Laertes does not *act* from the love he bore his father he is a mere painting of sorrow, "a face without a heart." Claudius is even careful to test whether this takes effect, by asking what Laertes would undertake to show himself a son in deed more than words.

To cut his throat i' the church

is the quick reply. No crime could be worse. It recalls Laertes' "I dare damnation" and aptly signalizes his returning fury. But on top of this there comes the dreadful news that his sister has just drowned. The brevity of Laertes' words on hearing this and his quick exit dramatically convey that his emotion at this point cannot be adequately demonstrated; it can only be imagined. The towering fury which Shakespeare has so exhaustively portrayed prior to this juncture, receives such startling new addition that no speech could do it justice.

Now, this is the person who grapples with Hamlet in the graveyard and who is brought to silence by the angry words that follow, an effect Claudius vainly sought to bring about by a craven lowering of kingly dignity. Laertes grew less turbulent with Claudius only when he, Laertes, calmed down of his own accord. But here it is Hamlet that brings about the calm—if calm it can be called—and flays Laertes with two noteworthy falsities: first, that his love for his sister is more rant than substance (certainly nothing as deep as Hamlet's for her), and second, his attempt to die with her is a piece of exaggerated emotionalism which Hamlet defies him to substantiate.

Between the empty ranter and the true-speaking man there are many categories. If Laertes were nothing more than a poseur, it is probable he would have been more conscious of the inconsistencies of his actions and would have tried to cover himself by retorting to Hamlet. But this he does not do. He is actually too noble for that. Not only the strength of manner, but the truth of Hamlet's words silences him. Laertes is not consciously false. He is too carried away by his own passions, and only Hamlet's explosive volleys can jolt his headlong fanaticism and gives him pause. If Laertes had ever entertained sincere doubts as to his sister being loved by Hamlet, they are shaken now as the Prince cries out

> I loved Ophelia. Forty thousand brothers
> Could not, with all their quantity of love,
> Make up my sum.

Nor can he remain entirely unmoved when Hamlet's rage has abated somewhat and he says

> What is the reason that you use me thus?
> I loved you ever.

The persuasiveness of this is not lessened by the cutting remark with which Hamlet follows it. While he is still resentful over what he regards as uncalled-for treatment at the hands of Laertes, there is no reason to doubt that Hamlet had always held in high esteem this man whom, earlier in the same scene, he pronounced "a very noble youth." Laertes' silence is meaningful, as are all Shakespeare's silences that seem to be out of keeping with the character or with the occasion in which they occur.

As is true of the silence of Horatio, nothing need be read into what Laertes fails to say. All that is necessary is to interpret the relevant indications which *are* brought out, and brought out clearly. The first of these comes just prior to the duel in the final scene. As the two men meet— their first meeting since the fiery quarrel at the grave— the King bids the two men shake hands. Hamlet then asks Laertes to pardon the wrong he has done him:

> Give me your pardon, sir. I've done you wrong,
> But pardon 't, as you are a gentleman.
> This presence knows,
> And you must needs have heard, how I am punished
> With sore distraction. What I have done
> That might your nature, honor, and exception
> Roughly awake, I here proclaim was madness.
> Was't Hamlet wronged Laertes? Never Hamlet.
> If Hamlet from himself be ta'en away,
> And when he's not himself does wrong Laertes,
> Then Hamlet does it not, Hamlet denies it.

Who does it, then? His madness. If 't be so,
Hamlet is of the faction that is wronged,
His madness is poor Hamlet's enemy.
Sir, in this audience
Let my disclaiming from a purposed evil
Free me so far in your most generous thoughts
That I have shot mine arrow o'er the house,
And hurt my brother.

This is honestly said and truly felt. While Hamlet still must be careful of what he says in front of the King, and we may indeed suppose that this care prevents him from saying many things that are undoubtedly on his mind, so many secrets are out by this time that it is difficult to see any great need of further caution in Hamlet's remarks. In any event, this apology to Laertes cannot be conceivably intended as a ruse or a camouflage for the benefit of the King. While Hamlet proclaims his madness, though he has angrily denied to the Queen he was mad, he is evidently using the term "madness" here in the sense of unthinking rashness and not insanity. After he killed Polonius his own rashness was evident even to himself, and he realized as soon as the ghost entered that he had been acting far from the design put upon him. While he cannot very well say now he thought he was killing the King, he can say with perfect truth his act was one of madness and not a "purposed evil."

A gracious apology may easily have the ring of fulsome obsequiousness to it, but Hamlet speaks this while Laertes still has fresh memory of the Prince's behavior in the graveyard. Had Hamlet begged the other's pardon without that quarrel ever having taken place, Laertes would certainly have rejected his apology curtly. He who could vituperate at the abjectness of his King would not display any pacified demeanor to the man he now knows to have slain his father. Yet his reply to Hamlet comes close to doing just that:

I am satisfied in nature,
Whose motive, in this case, should stir me most

> To my revenge. But in my terms of honor
> I stand aloof, and will no reconcilement
> Till by some elder masters of known honor
> I have a voice and precedent of peace
> To keep my name ungored. But till that time
> I do receive your offered love like love
> And will not wrong it.

This language, while it may seem to convey a summary dismissal of Hamlet's apology without any disadvantage to Laertes himself, is actually that of a man who is impressed without being entirely swayed. Yet how, it may he asked, can Laertes say, "I do receive your offered love like love and will not wrong it," when he is planning to kill Hamlet within the next few minutes? And would it not be likely that in a friendly match with blunted rapiers —which this is pretended to be—Laertes would assume a friendly air? If nothing else it would allay any suspicions Hamlet might have. This would be a fair assumption if, in the duel that follows, Laertes gave no hint of changing from his avowed purpose to kill Hamlet. But when the duel has been in progress and Hamlet has scored the first two hits, Laertes, referring to his plan to stab Hamlet with the poisoned rapier, says aside, "And yet 'tis almost against my conscience." A few moments later when he and Hamlet both lie mortally wounded, Laertes confesses all and asks Hamlet to exchange forgiveness with him:

> Exchange forgiveness with me, noble Hamlet.
> Mine and my father's death come not upon thee,
> Nor thine on me!

Certainly these things are said from a change that has come over Laertes. It is not simply because time has passed and his ardor has cooled, since, as we have seen, a much longer lapse of time has failed to cool Laertes in the past, and that was before he had the additional motives of Ophelia's insanity and death. Nor is his final desire to exchange forgiveness ascribable only to that amity men often feel when at the point of death. His conscience troubled him before he had any notion he was going to die. The whole pattern of the slow-evolving change must be sought from the time a difference in his behavior first manifested itself—which was in the graveyard scene. It was Hamlet's demonstration of strength in that scene, followed by a calm graciousness in the present one, that almost succeeds in working a conversion in Laertes. Or we might better say a conversion is actually brought about, but not until it is too late. Nevertheless, it is a pertinent indication of what can be accomplished by an ideal character who has a consistent balance of strength and tranquillity. By accidental circumstances Hamlet has exhibited both at instances quite close to each other, and the effect on Laertes is something like a combination of the two. Even allowing for the tragedy that is not averted, there is something wonderful and complete in this change that begins just after he curses Hamlet, and finishes just a few seconds before his death when he calls the Prince "Noble Hamlet."

While Hamlet's conduct toward Laertes appears more defensible than that toward the Queen, this is perhaps because we view Laertes as a more formidable adversary and certainly lacking some of the personal charm Gertrude undeniably has. But this difference should not tempt us to dismiss the fact that Hamlet is wrong in both cases, and for precisely the same reason: his grounds are personal ones. He does not know of the crime against his life which Laertes and Claudius have concocted, nor does he consciously seek to work the improvement in the person of Laertes which seems to have been brought about. Indeed, Laertes' pronouncements as he lies dying,

> The King, the King's to blame,

and again, when Hamlet stabs Claudius with the poisoned rapier,

> He is justly serv'd.
> It is a poison temper'd by himself.

testify to what his sentiments would have been had he known of the King's earlier crimes. And his favorable reaction to Hamlet's assertiveness toward himself is proof of what it would have been had Hamlet directed that assertiveness toward a more blameable individual and for a somewhat less personal reason. For in the man of passion—presupposing a certain nobility—as in the man of perfect balance, there is an attraction toward the ideal once it is seen in its true light. But the man of passion must first see something like himself before he will look for more.

Lastly, let us turn to Hamlet's treatment of Ophelia. I have already covered most of what I need say with respect to this and there is no need to repeat it. My main purpose here is to connect it with the two instances I have been considering and to get something of a comprehensive picture from the triple exhibition. Although a case can always be made out for the righteousness of Hamlet's deportment and its beneficial results, I have attempted to show that any resultant good is accidental since Hamlet is merely giving vent to his own feelings and not striving to effect good in others. Circumstances, plus a certain nobility in the recipient of Hamlet's ire, determine any potential good. The question always before us is this: is such ire a worthy substitute for the lackadaisical procrastination Hamlet is usually afflicted with? From whatever direction we approach this question the answer is no. Hamlet's rages are, of course, convenient refutations to such theories as his being an indifferentist or a coward. But a greater importance is involved, a larger moral issue dealt with, as is most clearly and positively brought out in Hamlet's treatment of Ophelia. As in the other two instances we can understand Hamlet's state of mind so thoroughly as to progress far toward the point of complete justification, but without ever reaching it. With regard to Ophelia there is no question of good to be achieved. She is not one of the evil ones in the play. That she failed him, that she proved lesser than his idealized conception of her for all her sweetness, has caused him a severe disappointment, it is true. I am tempted to say "cruel" disappointment, since it must strike Hamlet as something like cruelty when she comes to return his gifts in Act III, Sc. i, but for the fact that Ophelia is conscious of doing no wrong. Her conscience is not disturbed as the Queen's is, and as Laertes' is toward the end. Her first reaction to Hamlet's outburst is wonderment, as is that of the Queen; but where Gertrude soon realizes (or cannot feign wonderment any longer) that there are "black and grained spots" on her soul as "will not leave their tinct," Ophelia never comes to any recognition or confession of wrong. The more Hamlet rants the less she understands him. His doubts as to her honesty make little sense to her, and as he raves on in this vein she calls twice upon Heaven to restore him. No doubt Polonius has partially convinced Ophelia before this that Hamlet is mad; he is always talking about it, and this meeting between the young pair has been especially arranged in order that the King may overhear what Hamlet will say, and so judge for himself as to Hamlet's insanity. But this would hardly account for Ophelia's utter failure to make any sense of his insinuations in this scene. Her pathetic speech after Hamlet leaves her is not a repetition of anything she has heard from her father, but what she has observed, or thinks she has observed, for herself.

Later, in Act IV, Sc. v, when Ophelia has gone insane, she sings songs that refer, in a disordered way, to the two things that have caused her to go insane: the death of her father and (as she believes) the falseness of her lover. Whether the meaning of her song together with the early advice of her brother and father, implies any actual misdeeds between herself and Hamlet or simply to her having listened to his love too quickly and without at least some show of maidenly reserve, has caused some conjecture. It is not very important since in either case she would be guilty, in Hamlet's eyes, of a too willing surrender and then a matter-of-fact return of his presents. The point to be noted in this latter scene, however, is that Ophelia honestly believes that Hamlet has abandoned her. If she is conscious of any wrong on her part it is that she believes Hamlet has lost his love for her once she has submitted to it, whether or not her submission went so far as the surrender of her chastity. This is a complete misconception on her part, for much of what Hamlet says is an outgrowth of other things that are preying on his mind.

The knotty problem of aligning Ophelia's varying reaction to Hamlet poses a question. If she thinks him insane when he expresses doubt as to her honesty, why, at a later date, does she take him seriously? It will not help much to point out that Ophelia's conviction as to Hamlet's insanity is expressed, not when he asks if she is honest, but a little later after he has raged in an incomprehensible manner. If he is insane when she recognizes him to be so, he must have been insane a half-minute before. Regardless of what facts the supposedly disordered mind was referring to, they ought not to cause Ophelia, at some later date, to impute deliberate desertion to a madman. Yet, if her insane song contains any decipherable evidence as to why she has lost her mind, it is that Hamlet wilfully left her after having made promises of love. And the only positive evidence she could have for thinking this, comes at a time when she believes he is unbalanced. My own belief is that, while at first she does regard him as mad, later she changes her opinion. The reason she does cannot be definitely pinpointed, though it would be well not to overlook the fact that, immediately after Ophelia's sorrowful speech about Hamlet's most sovereign reason being "blasted with ecstasy," the King enters and denies in front of her that Hamlet is either mad or in love. I have pointed out that in the scene in which the play is performed, Ophelia does *not* act as if she thinks Hamlet mad. She does think him merry and bawdy by turns, and this on top of his denial in the previous scene that he had ever loved her, could easily cause her to come to the belief that he had played her false and was ostentatiously lighthearted in her company to show her how little he cared. She is mistaken, of course, but she interprets as true what is after all rather bluntly put.

Hamlet's unjust suspicions as to Ophelia's honesty would have been precluded if she had only mentioned that in returning his presents she was being obedient to her father's wishes. Unfortunately, her father is listening to their conversation. It is easy to see why she shrinks from telling Hamlet she is simply carrying out her father's commands, because even if she were to do it in a manner not uncomplimentary to Polonius, Hamlet would be very likely to press her to say whether her father's wishes were also hers. She would then be faced with the dilemma of having to say yes, and hurting Hamlet, or to say no and endure her father's wrath. Hamlet cannot know these things. The only explanation Ophelia gives him is that the perfume of these presents is lost, and "to the noble mind rich gifts wax poor when givers prove unkind." To what could this refer? It is true that Hamlet has not followed up these gifts and the many tenders of his affection, although some time has now passed; but this is because Ophelia has repelled his letters and denied his access to her. It is not because he has ignored her. Then why does Ophelia say what she does? Either her father has commanded her to say it, or it may be that she deliberately says what is not so in order to challenge Hamlet to profess his love. Such feminine artfulness is by no means unknown or unpracticed. If Hamlet could be induced to deny he had ever proved unkind and to insist he still loves her, the responsibility for speaking love would be Hamlet's and not Ophelia's. She would be guilty of nothing for which her father could censure her, and Hamlet, in addition to protesting his love in a way that even Polonius would have to believe sincere, has some power and influence as Prince to further their love. At least it would be a chance worth taking. If Polonius were still averse, the Prince of Denmark would stand a better possibility of overriding his opposition than Ophelia would—if only Hamlet can be gotten to declare himself, and she, by any receptiveness whatever, to indicate she will not rebuff him.

But whether Ophelia has been ordered to say what she does to Hamlet, or she says it to achieve something, I do not think she herself believes the literal truth of it. How could she? What reason could she have? We can be fairly certain of at least this much: she expects a different reaction from the one she receives. The courtliness of the age, the love which Hamlet has protested "with almost all the holy vows of Heaven," would not accept a lady's rebuff as the final word, particularly when it comes after a period of acquiescence. If Ophelia thought otherwise she would not tell Hamlet that his love has swayed her heart. This she does by letting him know that it was not alone the gifts he gave her, but

> . . . with them words of so sweet breath composed
> As made the things more rich.

She would be more matter-of-fact than to reply to his "I did love you once" that he had made her think so, and to his "I loved you not" that she was the more deceived. In her replies there is a note of unexpressed sorrow which Hamlet, if he were more himself, could not fail to detect. But this comes after she tells him her reason for the return of his gifts, and Hamlet's "Ha, ha! Are you honest?" reveals the first explanation a perplexed and overstrained mind can arrive at. Once having broached so brutal an opinion in the snapping of his control under the stress of immediate circumstances, Hamlet gives way to a torrent of abuse that pours over the bewildered girl like the ravings of a madman. Only when he becomes utterly incoherent to her does she think him insane, and this thought, as I say, we have strong reasons for believing she discards afterward.

Now, these three rages of the Prince can be seen in some sort of relationship to one another. By Ophelia he is hurt, by Gertrude he is both hurt and revolted, by Laertes he is challenged. He meets all three on grounds something like their own; that is, he ceases to be a passive idealist and becomes active—and in so doing descends further from the ideal—to hurt Ophelia, to hurt and revolt his mother, and to meet Laertes' challenge. All the while true evil goes unpunished. The failure to punish true evil is emphasized by a strangely similar relationship Hamlet happens to be in with each of these other individuals and to the King at each particular time in the play. His treatment of Ophelia comes of imperfect knowledge of all the facts that relate to her behavior, even while he is engaged in securing proof about the King; his treatment of his mother is based on proof which is positive enough, but this treatment comes after he has secured the proof he needs as to the King's guilt. His braving the fury of Laertes comes after he has received a greater challenge: the attempt by the King on Hamlet's own life. Shakespeare balances the appearance of each passionate action by the Prince, with a particular dramatic development that shows that action to be misplaced. The parallels are too consistent to be accidental, and each time we see him taking a course divergent from the proper one.

It is truly said that what a man really worships, that is his actual religion whether or not it be the religion he professes. It is equally true that what a man condemns is his devil, whether it be the real one or some inferior devil that prods him to personal recrimination. In each case man will be led astray. Like so many men, Hamlet has not diverted his attention completely from the true evil; but he is time and again drawn into active dispute with minor yet closer evils. It is not because Hamlet experiences any special sense of pleasure in doing this, though there is little question as to whether he gets a certain savage satisfaction from it. But there is a more intimate relationship between Hamlet and these others, one which arouses him to action on account of the personal suffering they cause him. He knows the Queen has done evil; Laertes is planning to perpetrate evil but Hamlet has no knowledge of it; Ophelia, whatever may be said against her love, cannot be charged with any evil either known or unknown to Hamlet. Yet Hamlet becomes equally vehement with all three, despite the wide variation in whatever can be advanced as justification in each case.

In the struggle with his problems Hamlet has slipped to the level of those about him, and even striven to outdo them. This may surprise us notwithstanding our acknowledgment of the stress he is under. He takes to retaliation quite easily, it being a descent rather than a rise. Observe what I have said before of Hamlet's moments of jocularity. He is jovial usually when the pressure of a step or a phase of his duty is over with. Not only does this demonstrate an uncontrollable sense of relief, but it presages for us the difficulty Hamlet will have in setting himself once more to his task. This relief, this sense of relaxed tension, is not seen in any of the three instances discussed in this chapter. The ghost must stop him in the scene with his mother. Those standing around must calm him by Ophelia's grave. And while he voluntarily leaves Ophelia, it is not because he has grown calm again; right up to the moment he leaves he is in a rage. In other words, Hamlet shows no disposition to halt when he is satisfying personal spleen as he does when pushed to carry forward his mission.

However, this much may be said in extenuation: as severely as Hamlet is hurt he does not lapse into a continuing and burning resentment. He apologizes to Laertes. After Ophelia's death he shows that love, not hate, survives in the one she wounded. While his feeling against his mother is of longer duration, this is because the way in which she hurts him is protracted by her living with Claudius. His actual violence toward her evaporates with the appearance of the ghost, and the admonition he speaks through the rest of the scene is for her own good and devoid of any personal rancor. From the greater evil of King Claudius Hamlet may be diverted, but the diversion is for a time only, and if Hamlet's condemnation of personal wrongs is more violent, his attitude toward the King is at least enduring.

VIII

CONCLUSION

To examine carefully the character of Hamlet is to see him in the wrong time and again. His individual acts and failures are such as to leave little doubt that they are unjustifiable in themselves, and when he is engaged in what we regard as right he manifests an almost subconscious displeasure that shows his heart is not in it. Yet, when all is said and done, who is there who can condemn him? To know him is to love him. Before we learn anything else of his character we learn that he suffers as a man, and we see this suffering continue through the various phases and relationships into which he enters. Some

217

of them intensify this suffering, others mitigate it. But even where a particular association is thoroughly agreeable to Hamlet, it cannot isolate him from others that either recall or embody what troubles him most. To understand this much is to begin to understand what he does and what he fails to do. His behavior will cease to be mystifying, as it often is to the casual reader of the play, and become more explicable. But even this understanding depends largely upon our seeing him in relation to a perfection he himself never lets us forget, yet which we must so often judge him to be short of. Unless we do this we cannot see why he is so weary of life in the first place, nor why other things bring about such paroxysmal reactions. We are reduced to dividing the man into parts that cannot be related to one another, or explaining all in terms either of a composite or of complexes which magnify trivia into enormities. Such theories are pointless attempts to ignore the basic reality of man's spiritual nature in a material world and the pertinence of that reality to the *Tragedy of Hamlet*. This is by no means absent from Shakespeare's other plays, but few are concerned so directly with it as *Hamlet* is, and in those that are the dramatic content is such as to be understood, if to some extent unappreciated, through a largely materialistic approach.

Macbeth is a case in point. One must recognize the soul of Macbeth in order to appreciate to the full the moral and spiritual degradation that come as a result of his crimes. But even the materialist is not mystified by this play. He does not explain Macbeth's sufferings in terms of complexes. The murders of Duncan and Banquo are so serious and so prominent that there is no need to go seeking answers for Macbeth's mental turmoil. But when the same method is applied to *Hamlet* only an insoluble enigma and the most conflicting theories are likely to be the result. The protagonist's soul-stirrings are as profound as those of Macbeth, but for what reason? Where is there anything comparable, as causes of spiritual upset, with Macbeth's crimes? (There is, of course, the murder of

218

Hamlet's father, but its effect upon Hamlet is one of the most perplexing things in the entire play.) What could possibly be compared with Othello's mistaken belief in Desdemona's infidelity? Or with the treatment of King Lear by his daughters? Or the wars of Henry V against France? That Hamlet is a malcontent is little more than a truism and it leaves us with the difficulty, in view of the fact he is not a malcontent by nature, of seeking a cause as evident as the ingratitude of man in *Timon of Athens*.

The apparent disproportion between Hamlet's feelings and the provocations which bring them about is one of the most confounding things about the play and generally leads to conclusions—regardless of how they are arrived at—by which Hamlet is defended, or condemned, or seen as a victim of some kind. It may well be true that he is a victim in the sense that he is a victim of himself, but hardly of something outside. I am speaking now of what seems in Hamlet to be incommensurate between cause and effect. People are fond of saying Hamlet was a victim of his age's sense of honor and revenge, so much so that he believed it to be right while instinctively he felt it to be wrong. The conflict between conscious belief and subconscious feeling results in thinking without doing, i.e., the actionless philosopher who is subject to deep cogitations and occasional outbursts of strained temperament. In the preface and elsewhere I have already given my reasons against this, but there is the additional fact that Hamlet is essentially the same before and after he is commissioned to mete out punishment to his uncle. That assignment aggravates; it does not create Hamlet's problem. Before he has even learned that his father's ghost has been walking at night he is in a state of intense suffering. The thing chiefly responsible for it is something to which Hamlet's world has given its sanction. How can Hamlet be seen as the victim of a desire to conform? "Conform" is a word none of us seem to like very much, and we use it when we find someone obeying rules we feel he ought to disagree with. Is the disagreement in him or in ourselves? Strictly speaking, everyone must conform with something even if it is entirely within himself, and if Hamlet can be properly said to conform to anything in this early scene it is to what he believes to be right. He is the lone exception in the gathering at court and shows no disposition to accept what others approve. If we feel the sense of honor is a much more persuasive thing than an indecorous marriage which may be condoned by the mores of the moment, we are brought back to the shaky ground I mentioned in the preface. If Hamlet has a true sense of honor there is no argument. To support the "victim" theory it must be in some sense false, and for this to be so the deeds of Gertrude and Claudius must be extenuated, if not outrightly condoned. Neither Gertrude nor Claudius are of a mind to do this, and no right moral judgment can do it for them.

So far as defending Hamlet is concerned, I feel he is lovable and understandable rather than defensible. At any rate he cannot be defended for reasons so palpable in themselves that Shakespeare would certainly have set them forth in the play *had they been the real ones*. There are reasons for our admiration of Hamlet and they are such that, while they may not bear direct expression, they are so clearly and continually pointed to that only by their light can we read his character fully. When I say that Hamlet's faults are themselves indicative of something incomparably better, I mean that we must be careful to see them as faults arising basically from a spirituality and the weakness that accompanies it in man. For Hamlet is never a wicked person. He kills one man unthinkingly. Two others he had put to death in self-defense. But he neither plots nor perpetrates any real crimes. He is not malicious. His wrongdoings are not those of Iago or Richard III. Nor is his weakness the cowardice of Parolles or the irresolution of Richard II. Both his faults and his weakness are evidenced in so many different ways that it is impossible to group them under one heading or designate them by special names. Cowardice, brutality, or what we label by those names, are there but they are there only now and then. The opposite virtues are there as well. In point of fact these designations are very misleading, and Hamlet's actions, contradictory though they be, do not merit either one. Calling him complex or a composite is an attempt to convert perplexity into certainty with a word. It only puts us right back where we were in the first place.

What I have attempted to show is that Hamlet's behavior is extremely variable and complex, but that it all comes from one persistent characteristic which we call imperfection. Anyone who does wrong is imperfect, of course, but we rarely think of the wrongdoing of literary characters in that connection. Coriolanus is proud and arrogant. Mark Antony is lustful, Shylock is vengeful. All of these men are imperfect, but we are less inclined to think that of them than of the particular vices which render them so. The pride of Coriolanus can be clearly apprehended without the additional thought that without his pride he would be closer to the perfect man. Or, to select characters more comparable to Hamlet, we can say of Othello and Brutus that they do appear nearly perfect except for one notable fault in each. Remove that one flaw and we have the ideal man. Here it seems that the central characters are near the ideal, one notch removed, and but for that they would be at the very summit. Such a comparison, however, is misleading. *Othello* is the story of the hero's love life. *Julius Caeser* is concerned chiefly with a patriotic endeavor to depose a dictator and set up a pre-existing republicanism. In the limited portrayal of each man, plus such secondary portrayals as Othello in the role of garrison commander and Brutus as a husband, we do indeed have near-perfections. The glaring flaw in each man is specifically a flaw his role uncovers. But if we were to see them in as many roles as we see Hamlet, would they still be limited to single imperfections respectiely? If Othello were a better judge of character he would be the perfect lover, not the perfect man. Similarly,

Brutus would be a perfect patriot, though very likely a disillusioned one. Consequently, when we use the word "ideal" in connection with these two, we use it in a relative sense.

When we turn to Hamlet these readily perceivable defects are somehow difficult to distinguish. We cannot see any great wrong, such as the lust of Mark Antony, which claims our attention exclusive of any comparison between the man guilty of it and the man of absolute virtue. Nor can we detect the one blemish on an otherwise unspotted surface as in Othello's blindness to Iago. Hamlet's deficiency is a many-sided, more comprehensive one that extends everywhere and manifests itself in ways which seem unrelated to one another. In literature this kind of wrong is generally that of the basest villain who commits every kind of evil and whose only cohesiveness is his criminality. The separateness of the different wrongs presents no problem of complexity as it does in the good man. For in the good man we perhaps feel that one fault is sufficient to make him human without destroying his innate goodness, as a multiplicity of faults would seem to do. The fact remains that Hamlet is the good man. He is at the opposite extreme from a moral depravity that can assimilate many wrongs.

How serious are these faults of Hamlet, and to what extent do they lower him in our eyes? That is a very difficult question. In view of the pre-conditioning circumstances which afflict Hamlet we have to say that the guilt is often lessened. It is impossible to assess the matter with any degree of accuracy, but one thing should be kept in mind if we make the attempt: Shakespeare deliberately avoids having his hero commit the type of wrong that has a deceptive grandeur to it. It is a fact that people sometimes see something admirable in a man who commits a daring murder, but they will never have anything but contempt for another man who slaps his aunt in the face. Clearly, murder is the worse crime. But whether its very seriousness lends to it a kind of impressiveness or the misplaced courage that perpetrates it engenders an equally misplaced approval, the greater deed is not likely to be so universally condemned as the lesser one. Hamlet is not guilty of any thoroughly contemptible wrong, but neither is he guilty of anything that, once seen as wrong, can be admired. Many have seen his procrastination as a perfectly defensible delay for one reason or another. But if they are right and the reasons are sound, there is no procrastination at all. If we agree that Hamlet does actually shirk and that this becomes clear even to himself on several different occasions, the wrong is established for what it is and in no way can it be made a thing of greatness.

When we see all these things clearly we find in Hamlet, even as Horatio does, a beauty in some way related to the very faults that would seem to deny it. This is only another way of saying what I have all along been insisting upon. Hamlet is not attractive to us *in spite of* whatever we find to criticize in him. If he were, then there would be a very important something in the play quite apart from his faults and which the faults themselves could not overbalance. That is what we mean when we say we love someone in spite of his faults. But if we scrutinize the play in search of a "something else," we find comparatively little and what we do find would hardly render him very attractive. The sympathy we feel for him as we recognize his distressing sorrow in the first soliloquy, our possible admiration when he bravely follows the ghost, are all to the good. His advice to the players betokens a discriminating taste in theatrical arts and, by possible inference, other arts as well. We approve his honesty in twice admitting to himself he has failed to pursue his duty, and we can admire his bravery in the final scene of the play. I have pointed out these things myself in attempting to arrive at something like a true estimate of Hamlet's character, and I am not now going to relegate them to a position of insignificance. But conceding their importance in one respect cannot make them important in another.

If we separate them from what I have pointed out as faults and attempt to balance a Hamlet we admire against a Hamlet we denounce, we shall never succeed in rationalizing what we instinctively feel to be there. These worthy attributes will simply not explain it. They help tremendously when read in connection with Hamlet's failings but that is a very different thing from reading them in opposition or contradistinction.

In the second place, we do not love Hamlet *on account of* his faults, as we often say we love certain people. Regardless of how they may aid our insight into deeper realities, we do not love the faults themselves. No one can be attracted to what he disapproves of except by way of temptation, and this would certainly not be true of anyone's attitude toward *Hamlet*. But because there is a close connection between Hamlet's faults and that loftiness they indicate, the attempt is often made to render them virtues and so make them lovable in themselves. The justification of Hamlet's long delay in punishing Claudius, or the attempt to convert it into an idealistic abhorrence of eye-for-an-eye vindictiveness, are cases in point. Such views present widely different conceptions of the Prince, but they stem from the same general impulse: to fashion him into something we can approve of because we like him in the first place. There are, of course, numerous people who have not attempted this, but in the absence of some adduceable entity that can be loved the "riddle" of Hamlet will always emerge with its attraction that cannot be differentiated from a succession of violences, delays, and contemplations of suicide. What is invariably overlooked is that the mere fact we feel called upon to justify him presupposes an affection that influences us when we come to something that can be called in question. Hamlet's thundering at Ophelia may be thought a well-merited reproof for her treatment of him. Even if it were it would vindicate rather than elevate Hamlet. But whether it is or not, the attempt to make it so denotes a predisposition that has sensed Hamlet's nobility in some other way.

All this is said of those—and I think they are in the majority—who find the Prince noble. There are those who do not, and if these are undeniably right in denouncing his wrongful acts we shall have, perhaps, a more difficult task in proving they are mistaken in their judgments. For that cannot be done by refuting the case against Hamlet. The case cannot be refuted. I have not attempted to do so, but on the contrary have pressed it all along. It is substantially lessened in certain instances when we realize that Hamlet's spirits have been scourged to the breaking point, and the result is a precipitation of these tormented spirits rather than an evil act coming from an evil mind. But wherever this is true the torment must imply the idealist who alone can experience it. The most obvious example of this takes place in the graveyard scene when Hamlet's intemperateness come in the wake of a deep concentration upon realities which he, unlike his fellows, cannot be unmindful of. The connection is always there, and yet it is the very thing Hamlet's denouncers overlook. Any hostile study of the Prince which I have read is incomplete. All we are told is that he does things he ought not do, or fails to do things he ought to do. Whatever does not square with such a view is either ignored altogether or listed under the heading of "Shakespeare's inconsistencies." Shakespeare was neither inconsistent nor careless in any of his dramas. He was a deliberate and painstaking artist. The way he introduces actions, the way he brings us into Hamlet's innermost thoughts at precise psychological moments, the careful manner in which he juxtaposes scenes, are decisive proof that he did not throw a lot of good poetry together without an overall plan. The play is so carefully planned that we do not have to strain after implausible reconciliations or far-fetched meanings; we need only interpret every smallest detail in the light of all and it becomes clear. It is more than coincidence that some of those who condemn Hamlet most severely as a character, also condemn Shakespeare as a dramatist. Unwittingly they are led into the very trap many a theatre-goer falls into who likes the soliloquies, Polonius' advice to Laertes, and "Alas, poor Yorick!" but who sees no comprehensive plan to the play as a whole. Shakespearian language will not be denied; but his dramaturgy? Consequently, the play falls apart and becomes just so many well-written bits, most of which work to the detriment of Hamlet's moral stature when analyzed individually.

If we are disposed to feel attracted toward Hamlet yet insist on a definite answer to what it is that attracts us, I cannot say more than I have said already. No quotation from the play will contain it, nor can any analysis adequately convey it. It is the soul of man we meet, and Horatio's silence is Shakespeare's own comment on it. It is a soul known only partially, but known definitely for all that. It is a soul that suffers, that weakens, but one which never loses its essential beauty. In it every man can see his own and, regardless of the differences in character that can always be noted among individuals, they bear some relationship to what we see in Hamlet. The weakness or the pain he is never wholly without are the origins of every weakness and every wrong a man will succumb to, regardless of how superior or inferior we judge any man to be. Noble in reason, in action like an angel, in apprehension like a god! The beauty of the world! Even in thought we find him essentially aspiring, though yielding to a defeatism, because the ideal existence for such a nature is not here and men are less than angels:

And yet, to me, what is this quintessence of dust?

It is Hamlet's forlorn summation of his soul's exile, but it can never be the final word with us whose profoundest reaction is one of surpassing beauty and whose final homage is expressed in the fervent prayer of Horatio:

Flights of angels sing thee to thy rest!

{ NOTES }

[1] Max Huhner, *Shakespeare's Hamlet* (New York: Farrar, Straus, & Company, 1950).

[2] Harold C. Goddard, *The Meaning of Shakespeare* (Chicago: The University of Chicago Press, 1951), pp. 332ff.

[3] T. S. Eliot, "Hamlet and His Problems," in *Selected Essays of T. S. Eliot,* New Edition (New York: Harcourt, Brace & World, Inc., 1932, 1936, 1950, 1960), as quoted in *Hamlet,* An Authoritative Text, Intellectual Backgrounds, Extracts from the Sources, Essays in Criticism, ed. Cyrus Hoy (New York: W. W. Norton & Company, Inc., 1963), p. 179.

[4] J. Dover Wilson, *What Happens in Hamlet* (Cambridge, England: Cambridge University Press, 1935), pp. 128f.

[5] Johann Wolfgang von Goethe, *Wilhelm Meister's Apprenticeship* (Dana Estes & Co.; Boston Centennial Memorial Edition), translated by Thomas Carlyle (2 vols.;) I, p. 274.

[6] Goethe, *ibid.*

[7] Huhner, *op. cit.*

[8] Salvador de Madariaga, *On Hamlet* (London, Hollis & Carter 1948), p. 24.

[9] Madariaga, *ibid.,* p. 73

[10] Madariaga, *ibid.*

PBO -8350